I0139735

BANG

Laura Shaine Cunningham

BROADWAY PLAY PUBLISHING INC
New York
www.broadwayplaypublishing.com
info@broadwayplaypublishing.com

BANG
© Copyright 2002 by Laura Shaine Cunningham

All rights reserved. This work is fully protected under
the copyright laws of the United States of America.
No part of this publication may be photocopied,
reproduced, stored in a retrieval system, or transmitted,
in any form or by any means, electronic, mechanical,
recording, or otherwise, without the prior permission of
the publisher. Additional copies of this play are
available from the publisher.

Written permission is required for live performance of
any sort. This includes readings, cuttings, scenes, and
excerpts. For amateur and stock performances, please
contact Broadway Play Publishing Inc. For all other
rights please contact the author c/o B P P I.

Cover art by Randi B Robin
First printing: December 2005
I S B N: 978-0-88145-300-3
Book design: Marie Donovan
Word processing: Microsoft Word
Typographic controls: Ventura Publisher
Typeface: Palatino
Printed and bound in the U S A

CHARACTERS & SETTING

Roy Le Fevre
Bev Le Fevre
Len Calendar
Sheila Calendar

*An underground condominium in Utah. The two room
"Mondo condo," a state-of-the-art subterranean luxury
apartment, is set into the strata of the Western desert,
somewhere between Las Vegas and Mount Zion. An earth
crust should be visible above the rooms, and the entire "unit"
should fit naturally into the geological formation. Earth tones
throughout should evoke the subtle shades of this location.
A bit of scrub grass, stone, or an occasional desert cactus
flower may also be visible along the crown of the set.
Lighting should be true to the colors of the western skies,
with special attention to the sunset, and sunrise.
The interior of the set should masquerade as a "normal"
one-bedroom apartment. In the course of the play, the
"Mondo condo"'s special functions become apparent,
and the walls and ceiling perform as a planetarium,
offering the "heavens." This apartment is truly a world
unto itself with synthetic seasons and day and night cycles.*

*The ratio of exterior (Earth, sandstone strata) to interior is
30% earth, 70% "living quarters."*

ACT ONE

(The stage is dark. The dimness lightens on the above-ground level, which is several steps higher than the main set, Unit B, the underground condominium. The interior, living quarters, is blacked out. Above, the entry area, is suffused by an ultraviolet glow: Sunset. A top crust is visible, crowning the set with a fringe of scrub grass, cacti. The geological layers are shown, as if in a cross-section of an archeological dig. We look into the rooms as if into a diorama: an underground room. Canyon colors evoke the Utah desert, the laminate of sandstone, subtle terra cotta and gray—the soft shades of centuries. Silence, save for the oncoming footsteps on the above-ground level. The CALENDARS appear, materializing from the sunset. They first appear as black silhouettes: a man and woman, heavily burdened. They can be imagined as timeless and primal: Adam and Eve in a parched Eden. But as reflected light gradually illuminates them, we see they are transported New Yorkers, anachronisms in this environment. They wear deliberately casual, fairly costly vacation clothes, and lug heavy tote bags, and two Zabar's shopping bags. SHEILA leads, LEN follows. LEN is tall and good-looking, wears metal-rim glasses. He appears abstracted, as he is alternately alarmed and amused by his secret thoughts. His body occasionally twists, conforming to a psychological warp. SHEILA appears, eager, intent. She too is attractive, with a forward jut. The CALENDARS have been married for nine years and function all too automatically as a team. They approach the upper level door, at a marital march. They

pause, as if before the door, face the audience. In tandem, they straighten, assume social smiles.)

SHEILA: *(With the vague irritability of the long-term married)* Get the wine out.

(LEN rummages among bags, produces a gift-wrapped bottle.)

SHEILA: I hope one bottle is enough. It was thirteen dollars. But it's worth much more. I got it on sale— it was...an incredible discount. She always gave me the five-ninety-nine wines. But she was single then. He's never given us anything, but we haven't known him that long.... *She's* the friend. And they never *stayed over*.... She did send us that cheese. The aged Cheddar.

(LEN whimpers, disturbed by her calculating.)

SHEILA: *(Misunderstanding his small sounds of discomfort. Re: the cheese)* It was a big one. It would have cost over thirty dollars at Zabar's. On sale. *(Concentrating)* But I'll bet that cheese was a local cheese. I bet they're cheap way out here. Still... *(Coming to her final decision)* We'll take them out to dinner at least once while we're here.

(She prods LEN, who holds up the wine bottle. They resume postures of social readiness. SHEILA presses the doorbell— a loud buzz)

SHEILA: *(Sweet trill)* Bev? Roy! *(Flat tone to LEN)* Did you tell them a time?

(LEN bobs in place, nodding his head to and fro in senseless agreement.)

SHEILA: *(Pressing harder)* Where are they?

LEN: *(Low)* They don't want us.

SHEILA: They invited us.

LEN: ...If they wanted us, they would have been here.

SHEILA: Do you always have to be so negative?

LEN: This kills it for me.

SHEILA: You're over-reacting. *(She presses the buzzer harder.)* Maybe they can't hear this.

LEN: I knew it was a mistake. It's always a mistake when I leave the apartment. Let's go. I'm not up for this.

SHEILA: It's just Bev and Roy.

LEN: *(Low but quickening)* They're more your friends. *(He contorts as if he might retch.)*

SHEILA: Oh, honey. Are you going to vomit? Please don't.

(LEN sways, undecided, gagging.)

SHEILA: If you're going to, do it now. Do it here. Do it on the Welcome mat. *(She squints, reading the mat.)* "Bienvenido..." *(With more bitterness)* That would be great, vomiting the minute you see them.

(On the lower, subterranean level, a candelabra appears lit. By this flicker of illumination, BEV can be seen: she flutters through the room—she wears diaphanous white gauze, with loose sheer sleeves that spread like wings as she moves, a moth-goddess, to light candles throughout the living room. At this point, the apartment unit is not clearly visible. The living room is stage right. Stage left is the bedroom, also darkened. The bedroom appears empty but a crack of light can be discerned under the bathroom door, far stage right. From under the door, visible steam: a white vapor—seeps. ROY LE FEVRE is within, showering. BEV runs to address her husband through the bathroom door.)

BEV: Roy! Roy! Honey. They're here. *(A gentle appeal)* Honey. They're here. You won't be long, will you?

ROY'S VOICE: *(Light, deflected by charm)* They're early, let 'em wait.

(On the upper level, LEN gags.)

SHEILA: Oh, sweetie! Do you want me to jam my fingers down your throat?

LEN: No. I want to go home.

(Downstairs, there is the sound of an increasingly intense shower: a hiss and more steam escapes)

BEV: Oh, honey! I still have things to do!

ROY'S VOICE: They're your friends, you talk to them.

(Upstairs, SHEILA shows her exasperation.)

SHEILA: This is just great. I wish you could have told me you were going to be like this. *(New concern)* Are you going to be like this with *them*?

(Downstairs, BEV becomes more insistent, but still sweet.)

BEV: Oh, honey! I have to let them in. Come out! You know I can't talk and do anything else.... Please... honey...

(Buzzer shrills.)

BEV: *(To outer door, for CALENDARS)* One second! *(Joyful)* I'm coming! *(To bathroom door, ROY)* I need you.

(Upstairs, LEN is twitching, swaying.)

SHEILA: Len, are you going to sabotage this friendship? This is serious. Say so, now...

(LEN is gagging, but not actually vomiting. He can't answer. Downstairs, BEV starts for the admittance buzzer, stage left.)

ROY'S VOICE: They can entertain themselves....

BEV: *(On the run)* Oh, be nice. Hurry!

(Upstairs, SHEILA moves bags with her foot, clearing an area for LEN to vomit.)

SHEILA: Is this what you want? Forget the whole trip. Drive two thousand miles back to New York? I'm not driving.

LEN: *(Brightening)* I will!

(LEN turns, as if to depart. SHEILA seems resigned to go, too. At the moment they turn, BEV buzzes the admittance bell. SHEILA spins, reflexively catching the door, pushing in on the electronic buzz.)

SHEILA: Come on. Quick!

(Lights further illuminate the stairs down to the apartment door. There is an element of the comic invasion to the CALENDARS' descent to the inner sanctum. In the dimness, BEV calls a final announcement for ROY's benefit.)

BEV: I'm letting them in.

(Outside the door, in the hall, SHEILA eyes LEN: a final inspection.)

SHEILA: Fix your hair; your fly's open.

(LEN simultaneously juggles bags, the wine bottle, reaching for his hair, then his zipper. He is only slightly awry, unnoticeably so, except to SHEILA.)

SHEILA: Never mind. You're fine. *(Delighted trill to inner door)* Bev! It's *me*!

(LEN freezes. On the other side of the door, BEV works the lock system, an elaborate electronic code box.)

BEV: Can't quite get this...al...*most*!

LEN: *(A last-minute whispered plea)* If they ask, my thesis is almost done.

SHEILA: *(Hissing)* The wine.

(BEV opens the door; it swings heavily inward. As she does, the lights illuminate the inner sanctum. Lit, the two rooms are suddenly visible, illuminated by roseate, recessed lighting, and the wall-sized "environment screen." The sunset, suggested by the initial lighting is now eclipsed by a more brilliant, artificial sunset within the condominium. There are no windows, only the great rear-projection wall that has the

*effect of an enormous "picture window." If possible, there
should be several auxiliary screens that later can be activated
to display "night" systems. The entire apartment can, by the
flick of a switch, function as a planetarium. At the moment
of the* CALENDARS' *entrance, this effect should be discreet.
The room is lit by a sunset glow, cozy as a "Southwestern-
style" restaurant. The two-room unit appears "normal"—
a comfortably equipped living room with kitchen and dining
areas, and a separate bedroom, with an enclosed bathroom.
The two-room condominium appears buried, like a time
capsule, in its subterranean setting. The earth strata remain
visible above and below the rooms, and contrast sharply to
the artifice of the interior. The rooms are set on view as if an
archeological expedition has ripped away the "fourth wall."
The home structure frame resembles a nodule, in its curved
wall, and the slightly miniaturized furnishings and built-ins
are reminiscent of a mobile home. The neatness and newness
of the rooms also contribute to this slightly synthetic feeling:
The rooms almost appear as if in an artist's rendering:
A few hyper-green plants hang in the kitchen, and there are
numerous "built-ins." A state-of-the-art media wall features
an "entertainment zone" and there are several athletic
devices also discreetly incorporated into the structure:
gymnastic rings hang on the ceiling, and a running tread
mill/exercise device, labeled "Ped-O-Power" is a permanent
fixture on the floor. In the kitchenette, there are many built-in
appliances, and cabinets, including two that serve a special
purpose: They can double as freezers, or, in the event of a
tragedy, serve as "morgue drawers." At first glance, these
special features should go unremarked. The room appears
inviting: The color scheme picks up the Southwestern
exterior, and there are a few hand-woven, Indian-design rugs
and artifacts in evidence. The stage is set for company:
candles, flowers, wine glasses, platters of hors d'oeuvres.
On the stove, pots simmer. From beneath the bathroom door,
the shower vapor continues to seep. A few details: Above the
dining area, a poster depicts the "'Heimlich Hug' First Aid*

for Choking Victims." A crochet sampler reads "Bienvenido."
As the door opens, BEV *and* SHEILA *fly into an embrace.*
Behind SHEILA, LEN *is almost inadvertently shut out, as the*
door begins to close on him. Unnoticed by the two women,
LEN *barely manages to make his entrance.* SHEILA *and* BEV
perform a ritual dance of greeting. LEN *stands, holding*
baggage and the wine bottle. He is almost inanimate—
a pillar of discomfort.)

SHEILA: You look beautiful!

BEV: *You* do! *You* do!

SHEILA: We do! We do!

(They spin circles, laughing, crowing. They pause, out of
breath, overlapping in conversation.)

BEV: Oh, Sheila! Sheila!

SHEILA: *(Eyeing the room)* This is terrific.... Very nice!

BEV: You don't have to say anything.

SHEILA: It's an experience just getting here.

BEV: Did it take you long?

SHEILA: Not *too*...

BEV: Did you get lost?

SHEILA: Just at the end.

*(*BEV *notices* LEN, *standing immobilized. Still embracing*
SHEILA, BEV *draws* LEN *into the circle.)*

BEV: Len!... Oh, Len! You look great! I can't believe
you're really here.

*(*BEV *kisses* LEN, *by accident, full on the mouth. He looks*
startled, but involuntarily responds, reaching out for BEV.
BEV *doesn't notice. Simultaneously, she releases him:*
he sways in place.)

BEV: Drink?

LEN: Please.

BEV: *(In high hostess babble)* Roy's in the shower, he'll be right out.... Let's have a drink—I think we have everything. Oh, here, let me take your suitcases... I'll show you where you'll be.... Oh, no, let's have the drink first. Try some cashews, they're dry-roasted. Oh, let me get some ice, it's cracked....

SHEILA: *(Snatching up nuts, following BEV)* Promise you won't fuss. It's just us.

(LEN makes repeated stiff-armed gestures to present the wine. BEV finally sees the wine, at the exact second SHEILA spots the hors d'oeuvres.)

BEV: Oh, champagne...

SHEILA: Chicken nuggets!

BEV: *(Ripping off gift paper)* Oh, it looks so... *(At a loss for words)* ...expensive!

SHEILA: Well, yes, it was, but we wanted to....

BEV: Oh, but you shouldn't have.... *(Flushing)* You wouldn't believe what we've been drinking... Roy likes the local wines....

SHEILA: In the desert?

BEV: *(Getting carried away with her excited confusion)* ...Yes! ...Oh, God...I can't believe it—You're here. I didn't think you'd really come. I thought something would happen. Oh, God, well, you found us! You can stay for awhile, can't you? I mean really stay....

SHEILA: You'll be sorry you said that. *(Accepting too firmly)* Well, we *will*. But you have to promise— We don't want to interrupt your schedule. You have to forget we're here.

BEV: Oh, we will. I hope you have good weather, but even if we don't...there's so much to do in here. It's just

so great....*(Dazed)* You really came. You won't mind
sleeping on the couch, will you?

(LEN and SHEILA zero in on the couch: critical)

BEV: It turns into a Queen. It's actually more
comfortable than our bed....

SHEILA: Oh, then you and Roy take it....

BEV: You'll have more privacy out here. The bathroom's
in our room.

SHEILA: We wouldn't mind that...Len?

LEN: *(Amiable, still smiling at BEV)* Oh, wherever you put
us, that's where we'll be....

BEV: You'll be happier out here on the couch...really.
Try it. It really is comfortable. I fall asleep on it all the
time without meaning to...I lie down to read and I'm
out like a light. *(Her face goes blank for a second. Reviving)*
God. It's so great. You're here. You're really here.

*(LEN, with an instinct for what will be his bed, moves to the
sofa, settles into catatonic quiet, his hand outstretched for a
drink.)*

BEV: I didn't think you'd really come. We're so far....
(Re: remoteness of area) Do you think I'm crazy?
Have I lost my mind?

SHEILA: It's a great space.

(Together, BEV and SHEILA tour the living/dining area.)

BEV: I got stuck with the color scheme—it was this
or avocado and gold. But now, I actually like it....
And the plants help....

*(There are two hanging trays of hyper-green hydroponic
lettuce, suspended near the dining table. As the women talk,
the audience should become aware of increased steam
billowing from beneath the bathroom door: The door opens
and ROY seems to materialize from the clouds of vapor. ROY*

*is naked, wet, his body draped discreetly in the mist. He
appears first as a silhouette: a male form emerging from this
"underworld," as mysterious a figure as the Ruler of Hades.
As the steam condenses,* ROY *becomes increasingly more
visible. The mists disintegrate and we see him as human, but
still impressive. He is a man of stunning physical appeal,
hairless as a statue and as well formed. His skin seems to
glow, a kind of marbleized shine. He has been humming a
tune, "Why Don't You Love Me Like You Used To Do?" as
he completes a cheerful toilette. As he swivels to dry himself,
it is apparent that* ROY *is totally self-centered, but what a
self: he's perfect and he knows it. At thirty-four, his body
reflects the discipline and delight he has invested in it.
He applies a lotion, then towels off, adding talcum to the soles
of his feet. He appears in high spirits. Also apparent: a virile
combativeness. He could almost be a prizefighter: middle-
weight. A slight tension in his body reveals his interest in the
conversation in the next room. In the living room,* SHEILA
examines built-ins.)

SHEILA: Everything's so teensy-tinsy and it all fits
together.

BEV: *(Re: built-ins)* You wouldn't believe what we have
in there....

(In the next room, ROY *opens built-in drawers, unpacks
several wrapped items on the bed)*

SHEILA: *(Stopping to study a picture)* I remember this....
You had it on fifty-sixth Street....

BEV: ...over the couch. It's the only thing I took with me.
...I sold the rest to the man who took my apartment.
Can you believe me, out here? Not even in Kreskin,
but *outside* Kreskin...me, in Utah! I bet everyone thought
I was crazed when I left New York...?

*(*SHEILA *indicates a denial: not heartfelt.* BEV *waves,
acknowledging there is justice in that attitude.)*

BEV: No, I know...I know.... It must have seemed as if I was being hasty...knowing him only three weeks... giving up my job, the apartment...leaving all my friends. On the surface, it probably looked insane.

(SHEILA *nods "no," another false denial.* BEV *performs an in-place two-step, her arms akimbo, palms-up, as if to concede or admit, "I know, I know".*)

BEV: People even said I was "on" something...I was! I was on Roy! (*Intense whisper*) I wish you could know him the way I do...I go to bed happy, and wake up happy...and it's all him, it's all him! I can't wait to open my eyes so I can see him, sleeping there, next to me...I'd given up even dreaming a man could be the way he is! He's the way they're *supposed* to be!

(*Aside to* LEN, *who appears discomfited*)

BEV: Oh, I'm sure you are, too!

(*In the next room,* ROY *grins, as he methodically fastens a series of leather harnesses and holsters to every conceivable section of his body. As each receptacle is fitted with the appropriate handgun or dagger,* ROY *smiles and pats the weapon in place. Within seconds, his body is criss-crossed by leg, arm, and torso straps: he is a walking arsenal.*)

(BEV *hops to countertop bar.*)

BEV: Is wine all right? I have a very quiet white wine.... It's light, a little fruity....

ROY: Maybe they want something stronger.

SHEILA: Wine is fine.

ROY: Len?

SHEILA: Len only drinks wine.

ROY: (*Lightly punching guests on shoulders*) Hey, hey... Mighty Sheila! Mighty Len! ...Made it all the way out here. None of her other friends, or so-called friends...have made it out here....They don't even call her. She wrote everybody letters, nobody answered. Out a sight, out a mind, I guess.

BEV: *(Changing subject in embarrassment)* Roy's been running twenty miles a day.

ROY: *(Lightly correcting her)* ...nineteen... *(To* LEN*)* You run?

SHEILA: He used to.

LEN: I'm slow.

ROY: Hell, I'll bet you're faster than I am.... Hell, anybody's faster than I am....

BEV: Don't believe a word he says.

*(*ROY*'s neck twitches: he eyes* BEV, *as if she's betrayed him.)*

BEV: *(Sensitive to his reaction)* He's faster than he admits. I tried to run with him and I was left breathing in his dust.

ROY: *(Mollified)* A mile in six-oh-two... That's not too disgraceful.... *(He grins.)* I *guess.* *(To* LEN*)* Finish that off... *(The wine)* and I'll show you the property while we still have the light....

BEV: *(Mild rebuke)* Dinner's almost ready.

ROY: *(Pleasant but definite)* It can hold.

*(*ROY *leads left to the door. As they exit,* ROY *scoops up the hors d'oeuvres, munches.)*

BEV: Those are for later!

ROY: *(With grin)* They were.

(Door slams behind the men. The two women, remaining, look to one another.)

BEV: *(Tolerant)* He's too much.

(BEV *grabs* SHEILA's *hand, pulls her into the bedroom. In high burble*)

BEV: Come in the bedroom. We have so much to catch up on. I wanted to talk to you at the wedding...really talk...but it was so crazy...I was in a complete trance....

SHEILA: *(More interested in the room)* What an interesting layout. Len and I need more space....

BEV: You wouldn't give up your apartment?

SHEILA: In a second.

BEV: Oh, I always loved your place.

SHEILA: Don't tell Len, but I've made up my mind. We're moving! I'm not going to die in that apartment. I have a plan: Just don't tell Len. You know how he goes on and on about that apartment. *(Bitter tone)* 4-R. It... *(She pokes her head into the bathroom door.)* What's in here? Was this made from some kind of kit?

BEV: A lot of this is prefab.

SHEILA: It looks like an airplane toilet.

BEV: It is. Without the charm. *(Intense whisper)* Tell me the truth. Was everybody sick of my getting married? Having to buy me gifts every few years?

SHEILA: We just hoped he was the one. *(She is snooping around. With more sincere interest)* Great storage space.

BEV: The whole place is storage! *(She slides open closet, produces clothing.)* Listen, I put some clothes aside for you...if you want them....

SHEILA: *(Grabbing a good jacket)* You're sure? *(She reads the label)* Bergdorf's? This looks like it was never worn.

BEV: Try the jacket. See if it's long.

(SHEILA *dons the jacket.*)

BEV: God, was that me? It's great on you. I have the sense that I will never need a suit jacket again. You keep it. *(Jubilant whisper)* I want to tell you something before they come back. You have to promise not to tell.

SHEILA: Who would I tell? I don't talk to anyone.

BEV: Not even Len. Promise...

SHEILA: All right. Not even Len.

BEV: *(In low, excited tone)* Sheila...it exists! It can be the way we hoped it would be...before we found out... it isn't usually that way. *(Pause)* I had to leave New York to find it. *(Pause)* He needs a woman several times a day...or he gets... *(Surprised pause)* ...headaches. I don't know if I can tell you this.... *(Instantly)* Do you know the Kama Sutra?

SHEILA: I don't read that sort of thing.

BEV: We're in it! Roy and I! On the male and female charts. The one that pairs up private parts. We're the highest mating...Roy and I !

SHEILA: Please don't describe his organ.

BEV: But it's so pretty! I never thought of one as pretty before...but his is! It has a kind of smile. Did you notice the way he walks? *(She struts.)* ...There's a reason! Everything about it is unique...I've never seen one like it...and I've looked...in magazines. There isn't another with its humor and its, well, dignity. *(She straightens up.)*

SHEILA: Are there a lot of them out here?

BEV: No! He's the only one. Did you think I was crazy to go?

SHEILA: I wouldn't personally pick Death Valley for a vacation....

BEV: ...but it was more than a vacation: It was a test. *(Recalling the trip)* "Upward Bound"..."Fourteen Days to

Test Yourself Against the Beauty and Brutality of
Nature...

SHEILA: I would have gone to Barbados.

BEV: I needed something...different...a real change....
The city was closing in on me.... You know how it can
get? When you see as if through too-strong prescription
glasses? The buildings too sharp, and overly outlined?
Everything converging? Everybody on the street starts
looking moronic...their eyes out of kilter.... *(She makes a
moronic face.)* It gets kind of Cubist...especially toward
summer.... You don't even want deli anymore. You just
don't *care*....

SHEILA: *(Thoughtful)* That's how it was when we left.

(BEV heaves a small boulder from the floor, displays it.)

BEV: I saved this rock.... *(She strokes rock.)* It was near me
when I met him.

SHEILA: Bev, it's just a rock.

BEV: Oh. Sheila! You have to understand.... *(She hands
the rock to SHEILA.)*

SHEILA: He walks on two feet.

(BEV looks hurt.)

SHEILA: Oh, he's all right. He's great looking.

BEV: All the women on the expedition thought so! You
should have seen us hotfooting it across the Mojave....
Thirteen women from New York...all divorced. Sheila,
I was *rappelling* after him.

SHEILA: That was dangerous.

BEV: I kept waiting for him to make his move...but you
know.... *(She smiles.)* He's really very shy....

SHEILA: He doesn't look shy.

BEV: That's a cover-up. He's so shy, I was afraid he'd never do anything. Then...it happened. On the solo survival test. I was supposed to go off...*alone*...for two days...to see if I could survive without food or water....

SHEILA: Oh my God. What if you can't? Do you get your money back?

BEV: *(Unconcerned)* Oh, I don't know. I guess you die. I didn't care about that...Sheila! Have you ever spent forty-eight hours totally alone outdoors?

SHEILA: I have no desire to....

BEV: Oh, you should! It's stupendous. The isolation is supposed to be the hardest part...Some people crack up. I just stared at the sky a lot...I saw the clouds turn to god men, their beards like cotton candy....

SHEILA: Were you hallucinating?

BEV: No, I was hungry. I was supposed to forage, but I just couldn't forage...I remembered something Roy taught me, how if you're too weak to hunt, you can attract birds by making kissing sounds on the back of your hand.... Try it.

(BEV kisses her hand; SHEILA obeys—half-heartedly.)

BEV: ...Young birds in the desert have no fear of people.... They'll come right to you.... *(She mimes a bird, flapping wings: Lowering her voice)* And you can kill them....

SHEILA: *(Shocked, accusing)* Did you kill birds?

BEV: No. I passed out. I just remember, all of a sudden, I felt...this *chill*...a shadow fell on me...I thought.. "Oh, it's a giant bird," but it wasn't.... It was....

SHEILA: *(Cynical)* Roy.

BEV: It was Roy! He'd walked all that way...tracked me.... There was no one, nothing...for miles and miles....

(She shivers.) I don't know if I can tell you this....
(Immediately) He was naked. We just stared at each
other.... It was a silent thing.... If we'd spoken, we'd
have broken the spell. We met the way men and
women met maybe a million years ago...silent and
for one purpose.... *(She catches her breath.)* I heard his
breathing change.... Oh, I don't know if I can tell you
this.... It's so strange. At the last second, as much as
I wanted him...I didn't. When he kissed me, I felt his
lips—they were so dry and cracked—the hardest lips
I'd ever felt, and I thought, "This isn't a *man*, this is
something that's stayed too long in the sun...some
old Gila monster going to devour me with his poison
tongue".... His tongue seemed unnaturally long and
thick.... It just kept unraveling.... *(She demonstrates—
Kabuki-style as if unfurling a ribbon from her mouth.)*

SHEILA: Oh, stop!

*(SHEILA half-jokingly buries her face on the bedding.
BEV re-enacts the scene, driving a dazed SHEILA backward
on the bed. BEV rests, poised, male-style, on her palms at
an aggressive angle toward the mesmerized SHEILA.)*

BEV: He held me down.... He had me at my wrists. I felt
his knee against mine...He made me open, and he broke
into me, broke into me the way men used to break into
women...I even heard a little voice at the back of my
head say, "He's breaking and entering."

SHEILA: *(Partially rising)* He forced you!

BEV: No! He wasn't rough.... He was.... He was...
the opposite.... *(She smiles.)* I kept my eyes closed...
I was afraid to look, afraid of what I'd see in his
face—you know how they can look— *(She imitates
routine male huffing and puffing.)* —but he kept on and
on...with this...this enforced tenderness...and finally...
I wanted to...see him. ...And there he was, smiling
down at me—the sun behind his head—he had a kind

of...corona. I could see his smile, his golden shoulders....
He was looking right into my eyes, as if to say: "See. It's
all right." And it was all right...wasn't it?

*(BEV, stunned by her own account, abruptly backs away from
SHEILA and moves to sit a distance from her on the bed.)*

SHEILA: I don't know. It's a bit borderline.

BEV: Oh, I've made it sound all heavy breathing and it
wasn't...oh, well, *(Amending with a smile)* it *was*...But it
was more than that.... Oh, Sheila, we just *fit*.... Even his
tongue made a kind of sense.... *(Confidential)* I don't
know if I can tell you this.... *(Instantly)* He can make
love with his cheeks. ...Have you ever done this?
(She imitates a cat-like cheek rub.)

*(On the other side of the stage, ROY and LEN return.
ROY appears boisterous, LEN looks pale and shaken.
The two women are too engrossed to hear the men enter.
SHEILA shakes her head "no" to the cheek-rubbing question.
BEV rubs SHEILA's cheek with her own; SHEILA backs away.)*

BEV: Don't be scared. You know I'm not that way.
It was just some feeling. It didn't come from me.
It passed through the room...like a breeze.

*(BEV doubles over, her long hair screening her expression.
In the next room, LEN and ROY stand at attention. LEN is
drawn to the intensity of the overheard declaration. ROY,
his face impassive, bristles. As LEN hangs back, ROY bursts
into the bedroom. His magnified shadow slices diagonally
across the bed, dividing the two women. BEV and SHEILA
recoil, a reflex.)*

ROY: What's going on in here? I'm starved.

*(SHEILA darts past ROY, fleeing like a spooked cat, to the
living room, and to LEN. In the separate rooms, the two
couples conduct whispered consultations.)*

ROY: I heard you.

(BEV *blanches, moves to* ROY *in a conciliatory way.*
He motions, with a crook of his hand—"Follow me,"
and leads her, on tiptoe, toward their glassed-in bathroom.

ROY: Come on, we'll be real quiet and quick.

BEV: *(Low, giggling whisper)* We can't. Dinner.

ROY: It can hold....

(As they disappear behind the sliding door)

ROY: Now don't scream when you go over...

(In the next room, LEN *and* SHEILA *huddle, whispering.)*

LEN: Listen, he's a little off....

SHEILA: She's flipped. I knew something was different
when she served us in plastic cups...and chicken
nuggets—*come on!* I bet she's using processed cheese
spreads....

(Sounds of ecstatic union increase.)

LEN: *(With increasing urgency)* He walked what he called
his "boundaries"...a half-mile in each direction. It's all
sealed off...wired. There are sensors in the ground,
electricity in the fence.

SHEILA: *(Matching his urgency)* She's in some kind of
trance.... It's like she's under mind control...*only lower*.

LEN: He keeps talking about something he calls "The
Shitstorm."

SHEILA: The what?

LEN: ...He says it's coming....

SHEILA: A Shitstorm is coming?

LEN: "Major." Major Shitstorm, Sheila. Part of what he
calls "The Megamess..." When everything, as we know
it...

SHEILA: A Shitstorm! A Megamess! *What exactly?*

LEN: "It will come in. many forms." He's going to weather it down here. Unless it's what he calls "a dirty one." If it's a dirty one, there'll be nothing left.

(In the bathroom, ROY and BEV are enjoying a tense, almost stationary union. Their dim silhouettes can sometimes be seen on the glass shower door.)

ROY: *(Loud, faked voice for the benefit of the guests)* Here, Hon, put this away, would you? *(Calling directly to the CALENDARS)* We'll be right out! Just putting things in order, here.

LEN: *(Hissing to SHEILA)* I thought it was strange they live underground.

SHEILA: That's for heat. It saves on heat.

LEN: Is that what she told you?

(BEV goes over the edge, emitting a series of soft, ecstatic cries. ROY moves silently toward his own conclusion.)

LEN: *(Overhearing sexual sounds)* This kills it for me.

SHEILA: *(Impressed)* Jesus.

LEN: Let's just go. Let's go back to New York...

SHEILA: Hold your horses. We *can't* go. *(Computing in her head)* Three days driving to get here...they must expect us to stay...at least two weeks.... Otherwise it's not worth the trip.

(Wild gasps continue.)

LEN: I can't be happy here. I knew I should never have gone out.

SHEILA: Don't be ridiculous. You're overreacting. Look. They're practically on their honeymoon.

LEN: I don't like this setup....

SHEILA: I know.... It's not any bigger than our apartment, but at least they *own* it. And there's plenty to do outside....

LEN: I knew it was a mistake to leave 4-R.

SHEILA: Oh, would you stop with "4-R".

LEN: I don't like this setup. I could have gotten a lot done, if I stayed home.

SHEILA: Even you admitted it was exhilarating to leave.... You said you got excited when we went through the Lincoln Tunnel....

LEN: Now I see that was a false exhilaration. My instinct to stay in 4-R has been sound....

SHEILA: 4-R is a dump! It's smaller than this place! I hate 4-R!

LEN: It's rent-stabilized—we can never leave. It has a beautiful view. I live for the sunsets....

SHEILA: Yeah, face the dying light of every day, if you want—I need a change of scene. I don't want to go back to 4-R. So, it's rent-stabilized—it stabilized at a pretty high rate....

LEN: *(In reluctant agreement)* ...like a patient with a low grade fever. You turned on 4-R, because we didn't buy it, when the building went co-op.

SHEILA: If we bought it, we could have flipped it.

LEN: ...not in this market.

SHEILA: Everybody else bought their apartment! Only *we* stayed on the non-eviction plan!

LEN: We were smart! We'd just be paying more to live in exactly the same circumstances. It's cozy....

SHEILA: ...as hell. Okay. This is an odd setup.

LEN: I don't like the setup....

SHEILA: But at least it's...a change of scene! *(Bitter again)* And they *own* it. And there's plenty to do outside...I'd have rather had the big bedroom. They didn't have to put us out here...I would have let the guests have the big bedroom. But we don't have to spend that much time with them.... We can just use this as a place to sleep and change.

LEN: *(Deeper whisper)* You don't understand. He's off.... He's *off* in some major way. He has this hyena laugh.... *(He gives a muted imitation.)*

SHEILA: I didn't hear a hyena laugh. He's just not a type we're used to.... He's from another part of the country.

LEN: I want to go back to our part.

SHEILA: We can't hurt Bev. I'm sure she's made preparations.

(She hears BEV moan in ecstasy.)

SHEILA: Well, we have to stay tonight.... It would be hopelessly impolite to go....

LEN: *(Tilting his head, indicating sexual cries)* What's that? Is that polite?

SHEILA: *(Becoming discomfited by animal sounds)* It would seem strange if we just left.

LEN: We can make up an excuse, so they won't be offended.

SHEILA: We can say you got a call from the college. You have to teach an emergency session.

LEN: *(Reverting to his main concern)* If they ask, my thesis is almost finished.

SHEILA: We could say you're sick. That's the truth. You *are* sick.

LEN: I'm not sick—I'm nauseated.

SHEILA: Well, you think of something else. But we have to stay at least for tonight. Bev will be crushed if we don't.

(In the shower, BEV and ROY finish their amours, then re-emerge to the living area. ROY looks pleased: he struts and SHEILA notices. BEV is even more dreamily detached than she was before the event.)

BEV: Forgive us. You must be hungry.

ROY: God, we're terrible, we're being just terrible hosts. Sit down, we'll have the chow out in no time.

(ROY moves zippily to kitchen area, sidestepping somnambulant BEV. The others, glazed, sit at dining table. ROY works with pots on stove: steam escapes —they have been at a boil.)

BEV: My salad has wilted; the leaves have turned black.

ROY: Don't worry, babe, I've got everything under control.... *(To guests)* Hey, hey...Mighty Sheila: Mighty Len! What'll it be? I have everything here.... Just give me your order, you got it....

SHEILA: *(Eyeing him with feminine curiosity)* What are you having?

ROY: Don't pay any attention to me, I eat like a maniac. *(He gives hyena laugh.)*

(LEN motions SHEILA: "You see")

ROY: I'm having some space foods...developed for the astronauts...send you into orbit.... *(Hyena laugh)* Nah, they're just real good nutrition and don't take up much space...here *(He indicates cupboards.)* or here... *(He raps his flat belly. He tosses silver packets onto counter, opens one and tosses contents into pot. He displays a one-inch-square foil packet.)* Compressed spaghetti: Can feed a family of four.

SHEILA: I'll have what you're having.

(LEN *looks askance at his wife.*)

ROY: *(Beckoning* SHEILA *to stove)* Come here, watch it
re-hydrate...

(SHEILA *obeys: walks to stove. As she approaches, the pot
appears to billow: a mountain of spaghetti foaming over the
brim.*)

SHEILA: That's amazing.

ROY: Developed it for the astronauts. I have a four-year
supply.

BEV: *(A bit vacantly)* And ten years of the fettuccine
Alfredo...

ROY: Yeah, we're well-stocked.... If the Shitstorm comes,
we won't starve....

(LEN *tries to signal* SHEILA: *"You see"...at the mention
of "Shitstorm."* SHEILA *is too engrossed, watching* ROY,
*who is preparing the meal with athletic grace and even
whistling and humming, as he works.*)

ROY: Hey, Len, what'll it be for you? Something a little
more ethnic? What's your background, I'll give you
your familiar foods.... *(He shoots* LEN *a look.)* Maybe a
couple of matzo balls?

LEN: No thank you.

ROY: Heh...heh... Don't be ashamed... Be what you are...
(He dumps dehydrated matzo balls into a pot.) Hey, Bev...
what'll it be for you? *(To the others)* Give the old lady a
break, right? Why should she have to plan every meal?

BEV: *(Dreamily setting silverware in place)* Whatever...

ROY: Hungarian goulash for you, babe... You love it.
(He dumps another packet. To SHEILA*)* What's your
background?

SHEILA: Just American...I guess...I don't know.
English way back... Maybe a little...Welsh.

ROY: I kind of thought so.... *(He whips out another packet.)*
...You could have the Yankee pot roast...or the steak and
kidney pie.... I want you to be happy....

SHEILA: *(Flustered by his direct gaze)* I can't make up my
mind.

ROY: *(Grinning, dumping two pouches in water)* You're
going to have it all.... Hey, Mighty Sheila... Why not
have it all? Huh? This is your first night.... Don't be
ashamed. It's an occasion. *(To BEV)* Hey, what have we
got to drink that goes good with dinner? Let's have the
good stuff.

BEV: *(A bit more alert)* I thought you were saving it for....

ROY: *(A bit too firmly)* I want it tonight.

(BEV sidles over to him.)

BEV: Then I need the key.

*(ROY, never breaking stride, while overseeing four bubbling
pots, pulls out a long chain, hung with a hundred keys. He
selects one key, gives it to BEV, who instantly drops to her
knees, crawls along the floor, whips aside a throw rug, and
uses the key to unlock a trapdoor. As LEN, SHEILA watch—
rather startled—BEV roots through the secret liquor supply
and pulls out a bottle of wine.)*

ROY: We got five years' worth.... *(Hyena laugh)* We'll
start tonight.... Open it up—babe...soup's on.

*(Still kneeling on the floor, BEV contorts herself, trying to
open the aged wine bottle.)*

BEV: The cork's stuck.

(ROY goes to assist.)

ROY: I'll do it.... *(Reddening with effort)* It's really in
there.... *(He takes bottle, smashes it against table edge, near
LEN's face.)* There, nice clean break... *(To dazed LEN)*
Let me get you a fresh glass...

(Paralyzed, LEN *holds up his hand, in fixed position, as* ROY *pours. Moving double-time,* ROY *returns to his simmering pots.)*

ROY: Chow time! Belly up! Grab a plate and get it while it's hot!

*(*BEV *rises, goes to kitchen area)*

BEV: Oh, let's do "sit down."

ROY: Buffet.

BEV: Not tonight. Let me serve them...I want to serve them....

ROY: I don't like to see you waiting on people... they're no better than you....

*(*SHEILA, LEN *look at each other.)*

ROY: ...and no worse either. *(He grins; his radiant smile)* This is the way we do it here....

BEV: Please let's do "sit down"...

ROY: Well...It's their first night. *(To* BEV, *with special tenderness)* You sit down, babe; I'll do the waiting on, if there's going to be waiting on....

*(*BEV *beams, allows herself to be seated.* ROY *bounds to his control system.)*

ROY: Hey, I want to play one of my shows for Len and Sheila....

BEV: ...while we eat? It'll spoil the meal.

ROY: *(Popping in a cassette)* They want to hear it. They never heard my show.

BEV: *(Whisper, to* CALENDARS*)* It was just cancelled....

ROY: Here I am. This is a good one.

ROY'S RADIO VOICE: Those who say we have no heroes, don't know where to look. A Sunday night. Couple flying their private plane over the Colorado Rockies. Husband, piloting the plane, slumps over... Heart attack.

(ROY *distributes loaded plates.*)

ROY: Go on, dig in. Listen to this: I'm great here....

ROY'S RADIO VOICE: His wife has never flown a plane. Does she give up? Quit?

ROY: *(Feeding* SHEILA *a forkful of pasta)* Ummmm... try some of mine.

SHEILA: *(Under her breath to* LEN*)* It's not *al dente.*

ROY: *(Seemingly oblivious, spearing* LEN's *matzo ball)* How's this?

LEN: *(Whispered aside to* SHEILA*)* This is unheard of....

ROY'S RADIO VOICE: By instinct, this woman, this wife, who cannot even drive a car, imitates actions she has only witnessed....

ROY: My voice is good here, huh?

ROY'S RADIO VOICE: The plane crashes. She crawls from the wreckage, dragging her husband's apparently lifeless body with her. A blizzard begins. She has sustained multiple injuries....

ROY & ROY'S RADIO VOICE: Two cracked ribs, facial contusions, a fractured pelvis, and a broken toe. Ignoring her injuries, she uses a nail file....

ROY: Go on, don't let it get cold....

ROY & ROY'S RADIO VOICE: To slice open her husband's chest cavity. She administers direct cardiovascular massage; in the process, warming her own frostbitten fingers in the heat of his internal organs....

LEN: *(Whisper to* SHEILA*)* I can't eat and listen to this....

SHEILA: Sssssshhhhh...

ROY & ROY'S RADIO VOICE: She keeps up her strength eating the only food she has with her: A Chapstick, three sticks of sugarless gum and a mint...Against all odds, this woman is alive today. Her only loss—the use of a frozen big toe. Small price to pay. No more heroes? You don't know where to look. This has been, "Nobody Asked Me...BUT". Nobody asked me...but! Good night!

ROY: *(Switching off cassette)* How was I? Great? I wasn't half-terrible, huh?

BEV & SHEILA: You were wonderful.

LEN: Your voice really carries. What happened to the husband? The "apparently lifeless" one?

ROY: He didn't have what it took. Too bad. It's a question of attitude. There isn't enough optimism in the world! People have no spirit! *(He tosses the pasta in the garbage disposal.)* If it ain't al dente, the hell with it! Make it all count. I've never eaten a food I didn't love...or had a woman that wasn't real satisfying....

(He samples SHEILA's *pie; she reacts.)*

ROY: Even the *worst* was wonderful!

*(*SHEILA *stiffens, stunned, as he nibbles her food.)*

ROY: Problem today is pessimism. Wonderful progress is being made, and all people see is the dark side. They don't see stuff like *this*.... *(He circles the table.)* They don't look at human beings on the moon, at pictures, close-up on Saturn—You see those rings?

*(*LEN, SHEILA *nod dumbly.)*

ROY: No. All they talk about are the goddamned problems. "Ozone." "The Greenhouse Effect." The Greenhouse effect! They never stop to think—"Hey, maybe it won't be so bad." You know things *grow* in a greenhouse.... *(He indicates his hydroponic kitchen garden.)*

LEN: *(Giddy to* SHEILA*)* The greenhouse effect won't affect him.

ROY: No, I actually look forward to it. I can see it as a positive. But most people keep pissing and moaning about all the goddamned problems: Pollution. Depression. Recession. Hemorrhoids. The threat of Terrorism, Nuclear War. All they think is—the end is coming up. The Big One is coming. The Shitstorm...

*(*LEN *signals* SHEILA*: "Shitstorm")*

ROY: *(Beaming)* ...and it is. But so what? Let it hit. It's hitting now. Everybody's fears will be fulfilled: We all know anything can happen and it already has.... Hey, you're from New York.... You've had a skyline adjustment. And the weather is ka-flooey. Florida will be frozen. Alaska will be a steambath. The dollar will fall. It'll be wheelbarrow time to go to the Safeway. It's all tied in—global warming whips up hurricanes that blow away your fruits and vegetables.... It's all been predicted. People, some people , go crazy. That's the vortex effect, of all the Negative Energy. When we all swirl toward one big black hole. Science and every religion predicts it—this is the season, the final season....

LEN: *(Whisper to* SHEILA*)* If he starts on *Nostradamus*, we're out of here....

ROY: Nostradamus saw it coming.

LEN: ...and his date for the end went by, didn't it?

ROY: What do you want? Exact accuracy? He predicted the Megamess, even the pessimism. How people view all this in a negative way...

*(*LEN*,* SHEILA *nod dumbly.)*

ROY: All they talk about is the goddamned problems. National Security, nonexistent— You could take out a

747 with dental floss! "Rolling Blackouts." "Ozone."
"The Greenhouse Effect." But...People don't stop
and think: You can use anything to your advantage
if you have half a brain, as I do. ...Things grow in a
greenhouse, huh? *(He indicates his hydroponics garden.)*
Genetically engineered vegetables and fruits...no soil
needed! I don't even have to fear a power crisis.
...No rolling blackout is rolling over me. I have my
own power. I can run this place by my own strength!
You'll see...I'll show you in a minute. Don't jump the
gun on me, huh! You probably worried, the whole way
you drove here about the goddamned gas prices...well,
I don't need gas—except my own! You know the magic
of methane?

(They make a face.)

ROY: People don't see the positive: they see everything
as the end, the Shitstorm. Hell, even if it is a Shitstorm,
I can harness the energy! The trick is to be self-
sufficient.... Sure, your fears up there will be fulfilled.
...The economy is gone now. What does a buck get you?

SHEILA: I paid six-ninety-nine for a pint of raspberries
and they weren't that great! I bought a four-dollar
tomato!

ROY: Can you deny a sense of acceleration?

SHEILA: I look at the price of hotel rooms, and no,
I can't.... But what about all this? What about
heightened global tensions leading to full-out war,
ending up in a Nuclear Winter?

ROY: *(Delighted, pleased)* That may be what we need—to
cool us down after The Greenhouse Effect. You have to
be positive, use your Positive Energy to counteract the
Negative. Be inventive: Create your own solution. You
can't say the destruction of the earth and the decline of
the dollar are bigger than you are. So what if, worst

case scenario, there's no atmosphere left? You think that's unsolvable?

(*Everyone looks stunned.*)

ROY: I don't happen to need an atmosphere. I have my own.

LEN: (*Holding his head, to himself*) I knew it.

ROY: I am ready for anything and everything. Ecological disaster, conventional or germ warfare, terrorism...

LEN: (*Caught up in spite of himself*) What do you think it will be? What form will it take? Another World War?

ROY: You want to know the truth? I *miss* the Cold War. We knew where we stood. There was them, and there was us. We each kept stockpiles. It was safer.

SHEILA: And there were so many good spy novels based on it.

ROY: Right! We had order. A non-war that worked. Nothing's safer than a standoff. Now nobody knows. ...One big cold war thawed into a half dozen hot ones... You don't have super powers, you got the stupid powers...the fundamentalist finger on the button. Those guys don't bluff.

SHEILA: They have such angry eyes.

BEV: (*Dreamily to* ROY) Oh, sweetie, you're scaring everybody. And they came a long way. Can't we talk about something cheerier?

ROY: This is cheery. Even if there are blowups, and major sections of the world are destroyed, there's no reason for pessimism. We always knew there'd never be peace in the Mideast. Someday, there'll be no Mideast—there'll only be an East.

SHEILA: Oh, I know. You should see what's going on
in our building—on 77th Street and Riverside Drive!
Every faction is working there now: The Albanian
super is fighting with the Croatian handymen for
control of our building's basement. Muslim against
Christian, Muslim against Jew...

LEN: It's the Tower of Babble, the cacophony of
tongues: Super against porter, porter against doorman...
They're down there in the basement, swinging fire axes.

ROY: Those argumentative little countries are going....
But we don't have to go with them. Even if there's a
Shitstorm, as there will, excuse my language, be...
I don't mean to mention shit as we sit down to a
delicious dinner—even if, worst case scenario...

LEN: You can count on a worst case scenario.

ROY: Okay, worst case, some pissant country,
descended from Genghis Khan, goes nuclear...
And let's say, a warhead lands near here, near Kreskin.
You think—we're all *vaporized*? Wrong. Wrong. Only
a few people will be vaporized. The rest of us will still
be here. Even the Big One don't do that much damage.
You know—you can even watch one go off, and your
blindness will only be temporary.

LEN: Swell.

ROY: Yeah! *Dazzlement.* That's what it's called. You lose
your vision but just for awhile, and then it comes back—
double, or with an aura. And only the front side, the
side facing the fireball, will be burned. It's even better
than that....

LEN: No.

ROY: If you're wearing white, or a print, you may just
get a little pattern burn. Flowers, or whatever. It's bad
to wear all black. Christ, we got to look to the bright
side. We can make it, if we create our own

self-sufficient world..."Limited" nuclear war. You know
what that means to me, Roy Le Fevre? *(He circles, feeding
on their plates.)* It means, it's limited as far as I'm
concerned. Count me out. This country may go down
the toilet, but I'm not going with it. The end of the
world is the end of me. It doesn't end 'til I do!

BEV: Roy's always thinking. If you stand near him, you
can hear his mind go....

*(ROY walks away from the table, as if surveying his indoor
"borders"—with pride.)*

ROY: Look at this place!

(Everyone's head swivels. ROY stalks the room.)

ROY: Look at it! It'll take anything but a direct hit!

LEN: *(Under his breath)* Or "a dirty one."

ROY: A hundred miles from the strike zone, you hardly
feel the jolt.

SHEILA: Won't the fallout...?

ROY: Fallout? Forget fallout! Fallout is nothing. You get
fallout on a loaf of bread, you just cut off the crust.
Fallout is a bunch of bull. You can hose it off the patio,
shower it off your skin. Just think of it as "dirty snow."
Fallout can't penetrate two feet of concrete, two inches
of steel.... *(He strides to the door, addresses it, softly, as he
would an unknown guest.)* You know what I say to you,
Fallout? I say "Fuck you, Fallout! You can't come
through my door." *(He raps the door, turns, beaming.)*
I have a hell of a lid up there, two feet of reinforced
concrete, a steel seal. First trouble *(He looks up,
demonstrates with a hand remote control.)* up there...I just
shut this place off. I can use "Touch-tone Security" or...
(He gestures to the emergency red lever.) do it manually.
Nothing's coming down here unless I want it to....
Nobody'd even know we're here. You know what the

lid says? It says "sewer." You notice the door?
And the hall light? That'll neutralize any spore...
"Spore No More". I invented it, like I invented so
much.... You'll see!

BEV: Roy has very original ideas...he custom-designed
this entire place! We have everything we need.

SHEILA: How long would you want to stay down here?

ROY: I'm glad you brought that up. If it were war,
germs or a nuclear accident, two weeks...but if it was
more of a social problem...pessimists finally coming
to their senses too late...I might want to stay down
here...indefinitely. The real problem will be people.

LEN: The problem is always people.

ROY: Right! I can hole up here for a long time. We have
four man years of food for the two of us, eight years for
one, assuming Bev will predecease me... *(Amending,
as* BEV *looks startled)* ...or me, her. *(Talking, demonstrating
special built-in "features")* Here are your food bins,
all good freeze-dried. I put the emphasis on variety—
I'd hate to be down here, on a monotonous diet,
getting bored to death...eight thousand gourmet meals.
(He holds up a one-inch packet.) "Whole striped bass with
black bean sauce, Hunan style." And you thought you
were far from civilization?

SHEILA: Oh, no.

ROY: S'okay. Your freezer drawers can double as a
morgue if you need one, though I hope to heck we
don't.

LEN: *(Whispers to* SHEILA*)* This kills it for me.

SHEILA: So quick to prejudge...

ROY: I've got life support systems, you wouldn't
believe.... *(He trots on the running tread.)* Ped-O-Power!
Three minutes a day, all the power we need.... I

generate my own electricity! I really *run* this place.
*(As he jogs, the lights brighten. He springs down, executes
some abdominal exercises.)* Great on the muscle groups
too—abs, pecs and glutes! *(He bounds off, to demonstrate
his unique equipment.)* We got to come up with creative
solutions! *(He gestures to an overhead thick pipeline.)*
Here's your purifying air duct.... Self-cleaning water
tap... Illuminating screen...for the illusion of non-
confinement... Back there... *(He points toward the
bathroom.)* ...is your Porta-Potty to get rid of, pardon
the expression, human waste...if the Shitstorm hits...

SHEILA: What if it doesn't? What'll you do with all this?

ROY: Well, hell, we don't need the Big One to be happy
down here.... We like it down here *now*....

(BEV and ROY nod happily.)

ROY: You know there's more than one kind of Shitstorm.

LEN: You're telling me....

ROY: ...The mega-mess! Banks can fail, but not me.
I have my own economy!

LEN: *(Muttering to himself)* You can't have your own
economy....

ROY: Self-sufficiency! *(He sees BEV doing the dishes.)*
Hey, babe! Put those plates down! Why should you
do the dishes? You're not a slave here, are you? Here,
let me.... *(He joins BEV at the sink.)*

LEN: *(Urgent whisper to SHEILA)* Listen, we have to leave
right away...we can't stay here. When I go to the
bathroom, make up some excuse!

SHEILA: We can't just leave...not *now*... I'm sure there's a
dessert. *(Lowest hiss to LEN)* Len, where are your
manners?

(LEN can't respond as ROY bounds back within earshot.)

ROY: *(Shaking his head in delight)* God, it just flashed on
me. How great it is that you guys are here. Seeing you
here at the table...it looks *right*. *(He refills their glasses
in celebration.)* You know, you're our first real guests.
We haven't done too much...entertaining. Weren't set
up for it. We're still not quite in gear, here, I hope you'll
excuse the appearance of the hallway....

(They nod dumbly.)

ROY: ...Can you keep a secret? I have a little confession
to make...when Bev said, "The Calendars are coming...
Len and Sheila..." I thought: "What do we need them
for?170

BEV: *(At sink, her voice mildly stricken)* Roy! *(To the others)*
He doesn't mean it the way it sounds.

ROY: S'okay, they might as well know. I thought:
"This is going to be really crummy." There are few
people I like to be in close quarters with...but I can
see already—it doesn't take me long—that with you
two, it's fine. Hell, you're real people, you and...
(He hesitates.) ...you and *Sheila*! The realest people
I've met since I been down here....

BEV: I just knew you'd all get along. *(To* LEN, SHEILA*)*
Roy likes people when he has a chance to get to know
them.

ROY: *(Beaming)* It's nice to have someone nice to talk
to.... Tell the truth, Bev and I don't do too much
talking...don't *need* to....

BEV: We have a very non-verbal relationship.

ROY: *(Lightly, half in jest)* Shut up, I'm not done.

(She quivers, he uses placating tone.)

ROY: We're real comfortable with each other in other
ways.... I just wish she wouldn't scream so loud when

she goes over.... *(Apologetic)* God, I was so sorry about that....

SHEILA: We didn't hear anything.

ROY: S'okay. It can get embarrassing, can't it? But it's okay...if you understand what's behind it—we can all understand each other if we just try: Bev is just a for-real woman...those are her natural responses to me...she can't help herself. Yeah, we're real comfortable together that way, but now you're here...I realize what was missing...Sometimes you don't know how you been missing something, till you find it again...and I been finding it here, tonight, with you...something I had a long time ago...something I had in Somalia—you know, that easy thing of just being together with good buddies you can count on for the long haul...face whatever Shitstorm is coming at you...as it sure as shit, excuse my language...is.... *(To* LEN*)* You're a real good talker.

(LEN's mouth gapes: he has hardly spoken.)

ROY: A real good talker. Everything you say makes sense. You have a brain, a real sharp way of looking at the world. You've opened my eyes to a few things already....

(Surreptitiously, ROY *touches* SHEILA's *hand, which is resting on the table, as she holds her knife.)*

ROY: And your old lady's sharp, too, and oh, God, yeah, easy on my eyes.

(He smiles angelically at SHEILA, *gently removes his hand—she starts, involuntarily tilting after him.)*

ROY: ...Yeah...I couldn't be more pleased you're here... than I am.... After all, with you here...it's...a social situation, not just me 'n' Bev goin' at each other....

(Charming wink to BEV *who looks miffed)*

ROY: ...In fact, this feels so right.... *(He gives* SHEILA *another surreptitious squeeze.)* ...it's okay with me if you *stay*... And I mean really *stay*...I don't even have to clear this with Bev: I know she feels the same way.... Huh, babe? We'll have Len and Sheila down here with us: I wouldn't have any couple but you...I don't even care, now you're here, it cuts our quotient in half...we factor down—instead of four years' worth of food for me n' Bev.... It'll be two for the four of us.

*(*LEN's *eyes roll in alarm.* BEV, SHEILA, ROY *share a toast. As they lift their glasses, a siren sounds.)*

ROY'S RADIO VOICE: This is a test of your emergency broadcast system. I repeat. This is just a test.

LEN: Should we get under the table?

ROY: *(Smiling)* No need. That's the beauty of being here. We're already under.

(Miming, LEN *indicates to* SHEILA*: "We have to go now!" He signs "He's cuckoo."* SHEILA *shakes her head "no." The siren continues.)*

ROY: Machine must be stuck. I'll turn it off.

*(*ROY *marches off to bedroom.* BEV *is busy at the cabinets, allowing a discreet distance between herself and the* CALENDARS.*)*

LEN: Let's go!

SHEILA: No! I'm not getting back in the car tonight. Besides, somebody has to talk some sense into Bev. She knows I can spot a jerk.

LEN: "Jerk"? How can you use a word like "jerk"? Whatever this guy is, it's more *major*.

SHEILA: She won't be happy here with him when the physical thing wears off.

*(*BEV *is working happily at the sink.)*

LEN: She looks perfectly happy. *(New tone)* Well...
You stay if that's what you're so hot to do. I'm going.
I'm not hanging around for dessert.

BEV: We have a special dessert!

SHEILA: She's confusing having sex six or seven times a
day with having a happy marriage. It's not the same!

(LEN stands.)

LEN: Tell them.

(LEN walks toward the bathroom.)

LEN: John this way?

ROY: Straight back.

(They pass.)

ROY: Oh, Len! One thing! Don't flush more than
necessary...we're...

LEN: ...saving water?

ROY: Yeah. God, you catch on so quick! *(To BEV)*
What's for dessert? I could still go for something.

BEV: Your favorite.

ROY: The ice cream!

BEV: Tutti-frutti. Hawaiian Ripple.

ROY: You won't believe this ice cream. It's
dehydrated...comes in sticks.

*(BEV roots through the food bins, searches for the ice cream.
ROY focuses on SHEILA, sitting right beside her. SHEILA
looks unnerved: attracted to ROY but still denying the
feeling.)*

SHEILA: Oh, I don't know if I should....

ROY: Oh, have some. *(Wicked)* I think you'll like it.

SHEILA: Yes...of course. It's not that....

BEV: Here!

(BEV *displays four sticks of substance that resembles Turkish taffy.*)

ROY: ...You're supposed to reconstitute it with water, but tell the truth, I love it just the way it comes.... *(He tears in.)* Umm...Try some...it's unbelievable....

SHEILA: *(Nervously munching ice cream)* Listen...something's come up. *(Pause)* Len and I are going to have to go.

ROY: Oh, no! We were just starting to enjoy ourselves.... The four of us! *(He glares at BEV.)* It was her, wasn't it? *(To BEV)* I told you not to scream while they're here... I told you....

SHEILA: No, it's not that at all. That was fine. We didn't hear anything.

BEV: Is it the bed? Is that it? Did you not like the idea of the couch?

SHEILA: No...

ROY: You could have our bed but it would put me out.

BEV: Oh, let them have our bed, it's no big deal....

SHEILA: No, no...it has nothing to do with you, nothing to do with this place....

(ROY *leaps to the convertible sofa bed, opens it.*)

ROY: This really is comfortable. You'll never know you're not in your own bed. Looks fresh sheets. And they're not permanent press, either. Bev ironed them for you....

BEV: I ironed them.

SHEILA: Oh, you shouldn't have....

BEV: I think it makes a difference.

ROY: Sure as shit it does! Smell this pillowcase....

(He tosses a pillow to SHEILA. *Then nuzzles; the pillow between their cheeks. He rubs his cheek against the pillowcase, a gesture that reminds* SHEILA *of the sexual techniques attributed to him.* SHEILA *leans toward* ROY, *and she undergoes an involuntary sexual tropism.)*

ROY: *Ummmm...* Can't you just smell the starch? Don't it make you feel clean?

SHEILA: I can...it does; it's nice.... It's not that.... *(Groping)* It's *Len.* He can't stay.

ROY: Ah, he'll get out and run with me in the morning, he'll be in heaven. We have it all planned....

SHEILA: Len is a very city-type person.

ROY: *(A bit sharp)* Is he a pessimist?

SHEILA: No! No...no! He's an optimist! He just gets weird ideas. He thought he could stay here, but now that he's here.... *(Gasping)* He finds he just can't.

ROY: *(Crushed)* I was going to show movies after dinner. I have a five-year supply. Eighteen hundred and two cassettes, and a thousand D V Ds. All good ones. This room turns into a four-sided T V, multiplex, my own. I often watch a couple of movies at a time. There's enough to keep anybody entertained after the Shitstorm. *(Brightening)* What's Len's favorite picture? I'll show it. "You say it, I'll play it."

BEV: Roy's favorite is *Shane.*

ROY: I love *Shane.* Yeah, it's one of the for-real great ones.

SHEILA: *Les Jeux Interdit...*

BEV: *Forbidden Games.*

ROY: *(Lighting up)* The kids in World War Two, burying their dead little pets...I got it! Len! You can come out now. I got it. *Les Jeux Interdit. (He flips through cassette library drawer.)*

SHEILA: No...it's more serious...Len...Len hasn't been well...since last summer. I don't know exactly what happened.... He was working too hard. He...he...strained his brain.

ROY: Like a hernia?

SHEILA: A hernia of the brain. Ideas were too heavy for Len...something...and now he suffers these little... brainouts. We've been to several doctors, they all say something different.

BEV: Poor Len.

ROY: God, I'm sorry to hear it.

SHEILA: One doctor says it's something called *Tic Douloureux*. Tic of sadness. He's fine most of the time, but when it hits, he can't control what he's doing or saying. He talks nonsense.... Sometimes obscenities— he doesn't mean them, of course, it's just a symptom. He could say or do anything.

ROY: Really out of control, huh? I saw a little of that in his eyes.

BEV: That's so sad...God, like what? What does he do?

SHEILA: Well, all right. This is typical. On the way here, we stopped for lunch at a Howard Johnson's, and Len insisted that we park the car at a spot marked for the handicapped...you know...the signs with the little wheelchairs. I don't know why. There were plenty of spots. I said, "Len, it's going to be embarrassing when we get in and out of the car, and people see we're not crippled. It'll look like we were trying to hog a spot close to the restaurant." He wouldn't listen. Okay. So we had lunch, and when we came back out, he confessed: He's been using their toilets too...with the

handlebars. He says they're bigger and better kept,
but I think there's more to it.

ROY: Sure as shit.

BEV: It seems that way.

SHEILA: There's something really wrong with Len.
Personally, I think it's totally linked to this economy.

ROY: There's no deficit down here. I've seen to that.

SHEILA: Well, just before we left, we stopped for cash at
one of those outdoor bank slots. I don't know how we
let it happen, but we were totally out of money, and it
was midnight and there we were on Times
Square...under a full moon.

BEV: That's when it happens.

SHEILA: So poor Len put his card in and the machine
spit back a message—"Transaction Not Completed".
(Her voice breaks.) It swallowed the card too, then spit
back another message, "Insufficient Funds." It was
embarrassing—there were people behind us. It affected
Len. He took it personally. It's too close to what he's
been working on...his thesis "Psychonomics...Going
Insane in a Crazy Economy." The truth is we've just
been squeaking by. We're close to broke. Our income is
the same as our rent. I worked it out on a calculator and
it costs us seventy-seven cents a minute to exist....

(Behind the threesome, LEN, unnoticed, re-enters the room.
He contorts in silent agony.)

SHEILA: That's why I had to sublet the apartment.
I hated to do it behind Len's back. But I found people
to take it for more than we pay, so we can actually earn
money by taking this vacation. We just couldn't go on.
I mean, the meter is always running. I have to buy
everything on charge cards. I use my American Express
card to buy milk. I buy all our food at Zabar's. We're

living on lox. It's eating away at Len, at his pride,
or whatever you want to call it. Most days, he just
sits on the sofa, shaking. He says, he's "quivering
from the cost." Every morning when he wakes up,
the first thing he says is: "Should I call in sick?"
And I say "Don't be ridiculous, what would you do
all alone in this apartment all day?" And he says he
wants to "concentrate." I know that he really watches
infomercials on AB development, or 911 cop shows.
He starts to...babble..."just-lemme-alone-in-peace-
and-quiet, just-lemme-alone-in peace-and-quiet".
To top it all off, he's almost totally impotent. He can
only sustain an erection in his sleep. I've found a
doctor who can diagnose impotence. A woman doctor.
A friend of mine. She's an expert on impotence. And
she's *offered* to strap electrodes to Len's penis and
record his erections over a twenty-four-hour period,
but no. He refuses to accept any help. Let's face it,
Len's in some kind of depression....

(LEN *is contorting, whimpering.*)

SHEILA: Len is in some kind of depression, and as
long as it lasts, he's no use to me, to himself, or to you.
So that's why we can't stay for dessert. He just won't be
much fun until he finishes his thesis!

(LEN *suffers; he throws a fit. The others notice him now.*)

LEN: (*In soft, strangled tone*) No one... Nothing.

SHEILA: See.

LEN: There's no one. Nothing.

SHEILA: He's doing it now.

ROY: Touchy.

BEV: Would he like a glass of water? Can I get you a
glass of water?

LEN: *(In quiet agony)* No one. Nothing. Nothing, no one.
No one. Nothing. Not a word...a moment...a look.
A look would mean a...lot. A touch would mean...
so much. Someone...something. Extend this night...
an hour could redeem my life....

SHEILA: See. He talks nonsense.

LEN: *(Quickening, desperate)*
"Just-lemme-alone-in-peace-and-quiet,
just-lemme-alone-in-peace-and-quiet..."

SHEILA: He doesn't make sense. He says one thing,
he means something else.... *(She eyes LEN.)* Oh, now
look. I'm sorry. He's going to start with the obscenities.
He has the expression on his face.... *(She points to LEN's
face.)* This is just before the obscenities....

LEN: *(Low, struggling)* F-f-f-f-fuck you.

SHEILA: He's trying to say, "Thank you."

*(SHEILA seizes the suitcases, takes LEN by the elbow.
Re-burdened by their luggage, the CALENDARS move
toward the exit.)*

SHEILA: Well, thanks for everything: I wish we could
stay.... In a way, I'm glad you're seeing this.... You can
understand what I've had to deal with...I thought a
vacation would help...being with people.... It was a
mistake.... *(She kisses BEV: a sympathy peck.)* It's all right,
it has to get better, right? Roy, thank you. It was great!

LEN: *(Low, to SHEILA, then ROY)* Fuck you. Fuck you.

ROY: You're welcome.

*(The siren blasts. Everyone freezes. ROY tugs the emergency
lever. Red light flashes. LEN lunges for the door.)*

LEN: *(With angst of one who sensed his doom)* Oh, no, no,
no...no...no... *(To SHEILA)* Sheila! Sheila! The door's
locked!

ROY: It sure is. It's electronically set. I kind of figured now that you're here...and we're having so much fun, you'd *stay*... *(Smile)* at least two weeks.

BEV: You don't really want to go. It took you so long to get here.

(SHEILA flies to the door handle. She and LEN grapple for the lever.)

SHEILA: *(Hissing at LEN)* Let me.

BEV: *(To ROY)* Sweetie...they're clawing at the door. Maybe they really have to go....

ROY: They're just saying that...to be polite.

BEV: Oh, stay!

(At that instant, the final thud of the steel surface lid can be heard locking into position. Everyone looks upward, realizing that the underground condominium is now sealed. Final siren sounds. Brightest light flashes. ROY stalks his domain, gives his hyena laugh, demonic smile. The following dialogue occurs simultaneously with light, sound effects.)

BEV: I guess now you have to stay.

ROY: *(Wild grin)* I insist! *(He opens his shirt—reveals his gun-crossed torso.)*

(Blackout)

END OF ACT ONE

ACT TWO

(The action takes place between three A M and four A M, in the pre-dawn hours of the following day. In the middle of the night, a certain surreality prevails; the mood and action follow the logic of a dream. Although LEN and SHEILA are wakened after only a few hours' sleep, they do not show fatigue or sleepiness. The extremity of their situation has them wired, alert but not fully cognitive. For the first several moments, they may appear zonked. The scene opens as they are seen asleep, two covered lumps on the opened Hide-a-Bed. The room is dim, with a pre-dawn "view" of the mesas, projected onto the Vista Wall. In the darkness, we hear the running treadmill, and the measured breath of an athlete: ROY, jogging.)

ROY'S VOICE: *(Low, ritual chanting)* I'm running farther and faster than they ever said I could...I'm running farther and faster than they ever said I could.

(The lights rise, with synthetic sun on the Vista Wall. We now see ROY in gym shorts, his hand remote control tucked into a holster. He has flicked on Country Morning system: Birds cheep. We now see BEV, with coffee service tray, standing beside the sofabed. As a pre-recorded rooster crows, LEN and SHEILA bolt awake, drawn reflexively together in their wakeup panic. There are several paramilitary magazines strewn on the bedding.)

BEV: How many sugars? Did you sleep well?

SHEILA: We took a little Zanax, Paxil and Prozac.

ROY: God, I had the greatest thought when I woke up...It hit me right away, that you two were in here with us. I didn't have to think. It was as if I was aware of you all through the night. It made for good sleeping weather. The four of us, breathing and dreaming together...God it warms the night air....

(LEN moans.)

SHEILA: Oh, Poppy!

(He awakens enough to remember he is furious at her; he pulls away.)

BEV: *(Almost leaning into bed with them)* Len?
(She indicates the coffee cup.)

SHEILA: Len's black.

(LEN buries his head in the pillow, ignores the coffee. SHEILA seizes BEV, tugs her down to the sofabed to listen.)

SHEILA: Bev, what is going on?

BEV: Don't worry. Everything will be fine. Roy wants a dry run, to see if his systems work. It'll be fun. "Fourteen Days, Thirty-six Events." Last weekend, he locked me in for a drill...Seven Events. It was...terrific.

ROY: Birds loud enough for you? They can be too loud some mornings. Specifically the bluejays. Don't they get squawky? What you're hearing is my "Country Morning" system.

(Roosters crow, seemingly in LEN's pillow. His head jerks up again.)

ROY: Dolby pillow, Sensurround bed.

(LEN, groaning, buries his head under cover, turns away from SHEILA, who is still trying to gain BEV's attention.)

SHEILA: *(Zonked whisper)* Bev...we have to talk....
You got to get out of here. We all have to go.
You have to *get a divorce.*

BEV: Ssssh. That's a little extreme. You hardly know him!

SHEILA: He's out-of-the-question.

BEV: *(Deeper whisper)* Give him a chance. *(She eyes* ROY, *running obliviously.)* He hasn't had an easy life, you know. The mother was a psycho. She kept him in a carton instead of a crib....

LEN: *(Turning, dazed but intrigued)* Really? That's so revealing...a *box.*

(BEV perches on the bed, very confidential.)

BEV: That was just for starters! What this man has had to overcome. *(Challenging them)* You'll see! Trust! By the time your vacation is over, you'll love him as much as I do! *(Half to herself)* I wish you could see how he lights up at the end. The corona...

SHEILA: *(As if the word gives her a headache)* No "corona."

BEV: *(Giving* SHEILA *her coffee)* Here, you probably want to get some of this in you, before you even talk. *(Deepest whisper)* I'll tell you a little secret. There's just one little secret to getting along with Roy.... Do everything he says. And never contradict him. And you'll never meet a sweeter man.

ROY: *(Swooping down on the* CALENDARS*)* I said: "Isn't it a beautiful morning?"

LEN: *(To* SHEILA*)* It's three A M.

ROY: *(Seizing* LEN's *expansion watch)* You're slow. Or you ain't on our time yet. P S T. Personal Standard Time. My Time. You don't need your watch down here. I'll give you the correct time. *(A beat)* A titwillow should be coming in about now. "Titwillow, titwillow..." *(Tweeting. fluttering his fingers, he bounds off.)*

LEN: *(With dull conviction, to himself)* I knew this guy was off.

SHEILA: The vacation is shot.

LEN: *(With a quiet, deadly glare)* The vacation?
The vacation! How could you betray me....

SHEILA: Oh. Poppy...I'm sorry....

LEN: Don't "Poppy" me. It's too late for that.
You...sublet 4-R! Strangers are in there, with my
personal papers, sleeping in my bed...reading my
private journals....

SHEILA: No, Poppy! No...I put everything away, in a
closet and locked it up tight. And the Lipshitzes are not
strangers. I know them very well. I trust them
completely.

LEN: How do you know them? I don't know them!

SHEILA: I know them from "group."

(LEN sags, she hugs him.)

SHEILA: It'll be fine. It's just for a little while, till we
get on our feet. For now, we better concentrate on this
situation.... Look at Bev. She's become retarded.

(BEV is happily cooking breakfasts.)

LEN: You can't become retarded....

BEV: *(Calling out to them)* Are you cereal people or eggs?

SHEILA: *(Hissing to LEN)* We have to get her to use her
mind again. She's lost her self esteem. We'll drive
her back to New York. They have support groups for
"women who love too much." There are millions of
them. We have to get out of here.... We might be able to
stop at a state park, and salvage some of the vacation....

LEN: There's no escape. Don't you see—this is major?

SHEILA: Oh, honey. I'm sorry. This is my fault. I'll get us
out of this. *(Calling to BEV)* I'm cereal. Len's hard boiled.
(Sweetly to LEN) I'm sorry...I ran off at the mouth a bit

last night. You know me. When I can't think of the right thing to say, I tell the truth....

(LEN, *undecided as to whether to forgive her, rolls over, clutches the covers, speaks to his pillow.*)

LEN: 4-R, 4-R...

ROY: (*Crowing, working the hand-remote*) Woooweeee! Look at that sun come up, over Santa Fe.

(*Blazing sun glares.* SHEILA *shades her eyes.*)

SHEILA: I'll get hold of that remote.

LEN: Sheila, you know nothing about electronics.

SHEILA: Kids do it in kindergarten. We have to get it away from him. Then we can control the security system....

LEN: You can't handle him, Sheila. He's too major.

SHEILA: Leave it to me, I'm better with people.

ROY: (*Soaring from the gymnastic rings, to hang simian-style over their sofabed*) I got a little formula. You'll want to try it while you're here. Every day: Something for the Body! Something for the Brain! Something for the Soul! Body comes first, because if that's not in shape, who gives a damn about the rest? Mighty Len...I'm going to get you in shape while you're down here...I got it all planned....

LEN: Oh, great.

ROY: You feeling a little uncomfortable here? A little out of your element?

LEN: No!

ROY: (*Kindly*) No, I can see how you might. Don't worry. I'll give you normal life cycles. What's your favorite time of day?

LEN: Sunset.

ROY: Mine, too. Want one now? I have a great Hawaiian Sunset. ...Or how about Twilight? Tahitian Twilight? It's lovely, Len....

LEN: No, no...thanks. Go back...I liked what you had on...first.

(ROY flicks on Santa Fe Sunrise.)

ROY: Sunrise over Santa Fe! Mighty Santa Fe! I'm running to Santa Fe.... Come on, Len. Run with me. *(He trots to treadmill, beckons LEN.)* Oh, I'm runnin', I'm runnin', I'm running to Santa Fe.... *(Calling to BEV)* Hey, babe, want some extra electric juice? You can grind those coffee beans.... *(He runs harder: a coffee grinder whirs into action atop the counter.)* The harder I run, the more power!

BEV: Oh, thanks, darlin'.

ROY: Come on, Len.

LEN: Maybe later. *(Under his breath to SHEILA)* It's the middle of the night.

SHEILA: Go on. Run with him. *(Under her breath)* He may get tired.

ROY: Come on!

LEN: Thanks, but I think I'll pass.

ROY: Would you rather run to Vegas? That's a great run.

LEN: I don't want to run to Vegas. I don't want to run anywhere.

ROY: *(Circling the bed)* But I have our day all planned. After our run, there'll be—Gun Quiz! You get a chance to look at those magazines I gave you?

LEN: I looked through *Gun Digest*.... It was very poorly written.

ROY: I never had any problem with it. After Gun Quiz, there'll be Breakfast!

BEV: It's almost ready, hon!

ROY: After Breakfast, there'll be Survival Drill, after Survival Drill, there'll be Snack, after Snack, there'll be Ninja Kill Sticks and Karate, after Ninja Kill Sticks and Karate, there'll be Psychological Counseling, after Psychological Counseling, there'll be.... Sex...

LEN: For all of us?

ROY: For some. After Sex, there'll be Music Appreciation.... Oh, no... Let's have Music Appreciation before Sex, then Lunch, and after Lunch, there'll be....

LEN: Nap?

ROY: No nap. Workout! After Workout, there'll be "Quiet Time," after "Quiet Time," there'll be Compulsory Relaxation, then Dinner....

BEV: You just let me know when you want dinner....

SHEILA: *(Hissing to* LEN*)* It's three A M, and she's making breakfast and he's talking about dinner. Whacko. *(Loud, fake, to* ROY*)* Sounds like quite a full day! *(Nudging* LEN*)* Go on, run with him. When I get him off guard, I'll give you the signal.... *(She demonstrates a chop hand-signal.)* Then you go for him.

LEN: It's no use.

SHEILA: *(Covert, seductive whisper)* Come on, Poppy.

*(*ROY *blows his whistle, looms nearer.)*

ROY: Gun Quiz! What's the best assault rifle on the market?

LEN: *(Low-key)* A R-15.

SHEILA: Good. *(Conciliatory whisper to* LEN*)* You know I'm so proud of you, I could scream....

ROY: A R-15! A life-saving gun! The man-stopper!
Very good, Len....

SHEILA: Len's a very quick study! He really retains!
(Sotto voce to LEN*)* See...I'm trying to make up.

LEN: Sheila! At least be...consistent! I can't take the
tension. We have to resolve this for once and for all....

BEV: *(Calling from kitchen)* Your egg is on! How hard do
you want it?

LEN: *(Low to* SHEILA*)* We can't keep fighting. We have to
get along, or give up.

SHEILA: *(Calling to* BEV*)* He likes it very hard. When the
yolk gets green around the edges....

LEN: *(Most serious whisper)* So I have to know: Is this a
vacation or a separation?

SHEILA: Len doesn't like goo! *(To* LEN*)* I love you.

ROY: A R-15... No exit wounds. Where do the bullets
go? Len? Mighty Len!

LEN: They just ricochet around inside you...bouncing
off your bones.

ROY, BEV & SHEILA: Very good!

ROY: Now tell me why that is, Len?

LEN: *(A bit into it)* The explosion is contained inside you.

ROY: When the Shitstorm hits, you'll be well-prepared.

SHEILA: When we get back, you can have the dinette set
as your office. You won't have to clear it for meals.
We'll eat on the coffee table....

LEN: *(Brightening a bit)* Promise?

*(*SHEILA *nods, kisses* LEN. *They kiss, automatically,
marital-pecking.)*

SHEILA: What took you so long in the john anyway?
If you'd come out sooner, none of this would...

LEN: You're not blaming *me! (Under his breath)*
I give up....

SHEILA: Why is it such a federal case every time I ask
for a little cooperation? *(Angry, she rises, addresses* ROY.)
Do I have time for a quick shower?

ROY: If it's real quick. Come on, Len—run with me.

(SHEILA *darts to bathroom;* LEN *shuffles toward the coffee
tray.)*

LEN: I don't see the point...to breakfast, to running....
What difference does it make?

ROY: You're a pessimist!

LEN: *(Soft)* I'm below pessimism...I live beneath hope,
but not above dread. *(Softest tone)* Oh. God, I wish I was
dead.

BEV: Have some coffee. You'll feel better when you get
something in you....

ROY: *(Polite)* Would you like a suicide pie?

LEN: A what?

ROY: A suicide pie. Guaranteed fatal in two minutes.
I baked them myself. Just in case there'd be someone
down here didn't want to make the "P" transition.

LEN: The what transition?

BEV: The "P" transition. The psychological transition.

ROY: It's practically painless. Maybe a little cramping
toward the end... *(Curious)* Well, we'll see. *(He moves
to food bin, rummages.)* So much junk in these drawers,
I can't find anything.

BEV: They're in there.

(ROY plucks out frozen pie.)

ROY: I'll have to thaw it out. You want to die right away? We can pop it in the microwave. It'll be ready in thirty seconds.

(LEN nods: right away. ROY pops pie in microwave.)

ROY: Ain't it amazing? Everything gets ready so quick.

(Timer rings: pie is ready.)

ROY: Here you go.

(He sets pie in front of LEN, who hesitates, mashing pie with his fork.)

ROY: There's basically two kinds of people in this world—survivors, and...the other kind. After the Shitstorm, there'll be only one kind. *(Re: the pie)* If you're going to eat it, eat it. Don't play with it.

LEN: *(On the pro-life side)* I haven't finished my thesis.

ROY: And *goddamn*, you should finish it. You have a for-real contribution to make. I heard everything you said last night....

BEV: He only looks like he's not listening; then he can give it back to you, sharp as a tack.

ROY: Everything you say makes sense. I don't think the truth is a disease. You don't need a doctor for it. You n' me, we're in tune. "Nobody cares"...damn right.... Except you, man, you got to care...for *yourself.*

BEV: You and Sheila still have each other.

ROY: That's your real problem there. I wouldn't take that crap from Bev for two seconds...No matter how bad shape your pecker is in, that's your business. We didn't have to hear it. Jesus. Being with her is worse than being alone, isn't it?

(LEN, encouraged by ROY's warm voice, nods.)

ROY: You want a divorce?

LEN: (*Quickening into involuntary confession*) We've separated twenty-seven times.... We just can't go through with it....

ROY: I can give you a divorce. I function as the state here. I have all the papers. Marriage... Divorce... Death certificates... Here... (*He drops papers in front of* LEN.) Here's your decree.

LEN: When will it be final?

ROY: In an hour.

BEV: I didn't know you and Sheila were having problems.... She always said you two were so happy.

LEN: (*Reviving*) That's part of the problem! She pretends everything is fine; Our values are completely different. We don't agree on anything.... (*Soft tone*) All that's left is our inability to leave. Oh, God, what if that's all there is to loving? —Not leaving? Some failure to inflict the final damage...severing ourselves....

ROY: And it's been a long time since you really got it on....

(ROY *turns god-like, incandescent.* LEN *is drawn in. Gradually, the women become aware.*)

BEV: Oh, look— Roy's crying! Isn't he beautiful? Oh, I hoped he'd be this way in front of you.

ROY: (*Flat, without looking away from* LEN) Hush up, babe, we're havin' a serious conversation.

BEV: He didn't mean that the way it sounded.

(SHEILA *sits down beside* ROY, *digs into her Cheerios. Their lower bodies are visible below the table.*)

ROY: Tragedy of most lives is people give up too soon.... They should wait—and give up later...when they're really through. What do you think I have them pies for?

If I'm ever less than I am now... If I can't do what I was born to do...think straight, run, make a woman happy... *then* I'll give up...but not before...not before. There comes a time...mine will be a ways off...when we each have to say it's over...but that'll be later, man: This is still your *before*. You don't have to kill yourself.... Somebody else'll do it for you.

(LEN *is enthralled. Meanwhile,* ROY *has slid his hand under the table and rubs* SHEILA *in slow, sexual circles. Stunned,* SHEILA *sits, spoon raised, her face registering total shock, and a degree of involuntary pleasure.*)

LEN: I have to admit: This is the first real talk I've had... I can't remember when..."You don't have to kill yourself...someone else will do it for you...."

ROY: We'll really kick some ideas around while we're here....

(LEN, *nodding, turns to* SHEILA, *sees that* ROY *is fondling her under the table.* BEV, *busy at the counter, has her back to the group, misses everything that follows.*)

LEN: What? Just when I.... (*Low, but final*) This kills it for me.

ROY: (*Innocent shrug, as he removes his hand*) I thought you were split. (*Raising his hand in innocence*) I didn't mean anything by it...it was just a gesture.

(SHEILA *twitches, offended.* BEV *swivels around, proffering* LEN's *hard-boiled egg.*)

BEV: Here's your egg.

LEN: (*Waving the egg away*) I'm losing my mind. This is impossible. (*To* ROY) You had me going. (*Wild*) Where's that pie? I want out! I can't take it, I can't take it!

SHEILA: Sssssh. Play along, huh? You can't seriously think I would be attracted to, let alone respond, to a man like him? You know what it takes to arouse and

satisfy me. Remember how long it took you to study the
books? I felt nothing but revulsion when he touched
me. I have to...pretend to like him. To get him off guard.
If I can get him close to me, distracted—I can grab that
remote, and we'll be out of here. And then I personally
intend to sue him. Don't question anything I do....
It's for you.... To make it up to you! *(Louder for others'
benefit)* You're overreacting!

LEN: Yes, I'm overreacting. Maybe death is an
overreaction to life.

ROY: Batshit! I've never seen a man more committed to
his own survival.

LEN: You know: maybe survival isn't the be-all and
end-all? Huh? Probably the greatest people are already
dead. God knows, I'm not the man my father was...
I'm not the man my mother was....

SHEILA: They died, one right after the other. When
Len was twelve. The mother had tumors the size of
grapefruits in her uterus. The father had tumors the
size of tangerines in his brain....

LEN: How could those doctors compare them to fruit?
It was so insensitive. You'd think we were a family of
citrus growers. We were all so close. I knew...there was
love—that's why this is hard. I don't know why I didn't
check out when they did. What am I hanging around
for?

ROY: You love it! You'd do anything to stay alive!
See this arm. You'd be snackin' on it like it was a
drumstick from Colonel Sanders. You scarfed up
the chow pretty good last night.

LEN: I won't even dignify that with a response.
And I would hardly say "scarfed."

SHEILA: Len hardly got a bite to eat!

LEN: *(Aside to* SHEILA*)* That's not the point.... *(Dead-on to* ROY*)* And besides, did you ever stop and think maybe there's more signs of commitment to life than the intake of "chow"?

ROY: It's an indicator. You want to die...then eat that pie.

LEN: *(Cute)* I don't like the idea of the "cramping." Anyway. I shouldn't thank you....

ROY: You're welcome.

LEN: ...but maybe I need this...to see what I'm against. *(He heads for the sofabed.)* All I ask is to be left alone. So I can concentrate.... It might not be a total waste... as long as I can concentrate.

(He creates a tent, using the bedcovers. SHEILA *tries to tug off the blanket.)*

LEN: May I have a little privacy here?

SHEILA: *(Lowest hiss)* Come on, Len, you don't seriously think I could be interested in....

ROY: *(Chanting to himself as he trots)* I'm running farther and faster than they ever said I could....

SHEILA: *(Very low, under tent-cover)* ...this clown ? You know I have to humor him....

LEN: *(Whispering under the "tent")* Was that all it was?

ROY: I thought you n' me were going to run together.... If we don't stick to the schedule, this place'll be a zoo....

SHEILA: I love you....

LEN: It's beginning to sound like a threat.

BEV: It could get sordid....

ROY: After our Run, there'll be Survival Training. After Survival Training, there'll be Snack. After Snack, there'll be Ninja, Kill Sticks and Karate.... After Ninja, Kill Sticks and Karate, there'll be Psychological

Counseling, after Psychological Counseling, there'll be
Music Appreciation, after Music Appreciation, there'll
be....

SHEILA: Sex.

ROY: Sex. God, you catch on so quick. After Sex, there'll
be Lunch, after Lunch.... No, let's skip Lunch... Let's go
straight to Workout...

BEV: Oh, honey, maybe they just want to relax....

ROY: They'll relax. We'll have Compulsory Relaxation
after Dinner...or, hey, why not combine them, and call
it a party! Huh! That's what we'll do, if we all do
well—hey, what do you say: A real party tonight!

(LEN *tightens his blanket tent, assumes fetal curl.*)

SHEILA: Len, you're not at home! Oh, go ahead, lie
there like a vegetable, pull the covers over your head....
(Leaning lower to whisper) Come on, darling, let's not
fight.

LEN: You're right. We don't even know if we'll last the
night.

SHEILA: We have to present a united front.

LEN: How can I give you the benefit of the doubt?
Oh, all right. But this is the last time, Sheila....
One more thing, one more remark, honest-to-Christ,
that's it. We're through.

SHEILA: Give me a kiss.

(*They kiss perfunctorily.*)

SHEILA: *(Whispering instructions)* Now remember the
signal... *(She demonstrates: a hand-chop.)* When you see
me do this, go for him and I'll get the remote....

(LEN *nods.* ROY *bounds near the bed.*)

ROY: Woooweee! Twenty-one miles! A record!
Oh man don't it feel good, ain't it great to sweat?

(He starts to close the sofabed with LEN *in it, forcing* LEN
to emerge from the sandwiching mattress halves. LEN *looks
to* SHEILA, *mimes—should they attack?* SHEILA *mimes:
No, not yet.* ROY *blows his whistle.)*

ROY: Survival Drill!

LEN: What happened to breakfast?

*(*ROY *tosses* LEN's *hard-boiled egg in the air, then swallows
it whole.)*

ROY: You just skipped it. You skip the Run, you skip
breakfast, too. Okay! Survival Drill! Bev! Sheila!
Everybody! Don't you want to learn how to adapt
to life down here?

LEN: No.

ROY: What I am about to show you will someday...
maybe even today, save your life. What're the main
dangers down here?

LEN: I can't even imagine.

SHEILA: Don't get smart with him. *(Louder to* ROY*)*
Oh, what are they? The dangers...?

ROY: *(Happy to relate)* Carbon monoxide poisoning.
Hypothermia. Electroshock. Acute illness without
a doctor present... Don't worry about that last—
I learned all I need to know from a veterinarian.

LEN: I'm ill.

ROY: Are you?

LEN: No!

ROY: How do you spot carbon monoxide poisoning?

BEV: Victim's blue, with cherry red lips.

ROY: Nice, babe! Okay...Len, Sheila...Electroshock Drill!
I'm stuck to an outlet....

(ROY *vibrates, as if his finger is stuck in a live socket.*
LEN *looks to* SHEILA: *Should he make a move now?*
She shakes her head, "No, later." BEV, SHEILA *reach*
out to ROY—*an invisible electrical charge links them*
in a make-believe electroshock "dance".)

BEV: Hold out a piece of wood!

(LEN *grabs broom handle, again looks at* SHEILA,
as if, "Should I use the broom?" She indicates, again,
"Not yet—play along." LEN *breaks the "current."*
The trio are "freed".)

ROY: God, you catch on so quick!

(SHEILA, *winded, goes to food bin, snatches up a few fistfuls*
of ice cream sticks, munches. SHEILA *should nosh on these*
sticks for the next several minutes.)

SHEILA: Len has an I Q that's higher than his weight.

ROY: Yeah, but bein' smart isn't the same as being
emotionally stable. (*He squints closer at* LEN.) He still
looks a little unbalanced to me. He's got that wild look.
(*To* LEN, *directly*) I don't want to hurt your feelings, Len,
but frankly, even on our short acquaintance, I can see
you're a candidate for Psychological Counseling....

LEN: What about Ninja, Kill Sticks and Karate?

ROY: Violent, huh?

LEN: I thought it was on the schedule.

ROY: It is...But looking at you weirding out on me,
makes me think you need Psychological Counseling,
before I even put a Kill Stick in your hand.... Are you
going to throw another brainout?

(LEN *looks to* SHEILA *again: again, no signal*)

ROY: *(Very patient tone)* You see, after the Shitstorm, it'll be a new society, with no room for the "granola heads"—"fruits, flakes, or nuts." It is even possible, there'll be ultimately no one left in your area, but you. In that case, you are your own society.

LEN: *(Low, exasperated, to* SHEILA*)* You can't be your own society....

ROY: *(Gently overriding him)* You have to feel comfortable enough in your own skin, so that you can go on totally alone, in a devastated universe...and still feel completely confident and happy! *(He claps his hands.)* Everybody! I want to see you all standing on your heads...the more blood is rushing to the brain, the quicker the head clears....

*(*LEN, SHEILA, BEV *assume Yoga headstand.)*

ROY: We're going to make the "P" transition.... *(He stands over* LEN*)* Len, inhale. Exhale. Relax the body. We'll solve your problems in a second. You've been going for that Ph.D. how long? Ten years? Len, it's taking too long...Those who can, do, those who can't, teach...Len, you're a teacher.... *(A beat)* Len, you've known your wife....

SHEILA: *Sheila*!

ROY: Your wife, Sheila, how long?

LEN: Ten years. We met at a mixer. She was the first girl I asked to dance who said "yes." She seemed pretty and sweet.

ROY:...and how many years later, maybe one night, you was at a steak joint, maybe you were a little beered up.... You went to the men's room and she went to the ladies' and when you came out.... You couldn't recognize her.... This woman came toward you with a funny look on her face, and you wondered....

LEN: *(Joining in, rapt)* "...Who is this woman?" When did her neck start to come forward? When did her voice go up so high? When did she start to say my name in sections?

SHEILA: "Le-*en!*"

LEN: ...when did my name become a whine? *(To* ROY*)* How did you know?

BEV: Roy really sees.

SHEILA: I don't like this.

ROY: *(Moving on to her)* That's how he sees you: *(Soft)* Not me. Inhale. Exhale, Relax the body.

(SHEILA *tenses, clamping her legs shut.)*

ROY: Sheila? How old were you when you married Len?

SHEILA: Twenty...*just.*

ROY: Your body was ready, your brain wasn't. *(Very gentle)* You married a nerd, and now you're Mrs Nerd.... None of your dreams is coming true, and the nerd bangs useless against you in the night. Everybody is better off than you....

SHEILA: *(With uncontrolled bitterness)* ...living in their expensive apartments, driving their brand-new cars...

ROY: After the Shitstorm, a lot of those apartments will be empty, and a lot of the cars, too. Some may be damaged or radioactive, but most of them will be as good as they ever were.... You'll have your pick. And think of them department stores, all them empty aisles...You'll be waltzing down them aisles, and no snippy salesgirls saying "Cash or charge?"

LEN: I've never encountered shallowness of this depth.

ROY: *(Soft aside to* LEN*)* This is her dream, man, you can let another person have her dream.

LEN: I'll tell you something. Her shopping has always scared me. I don't know how you pick up on these things, but that's a big factor, a big factor. I don't know why, but sometimes she doesn't even unwrap her packages...I find them in closets, stapled with receipts.... *(He shudders, terrified.)* We go to...malls...so she can get more. I'm scared someday I'll die at a mall, and I'll be described as a "dead shopper."

ROY: I hear you. I never wanted to be a "dead motorist." *(He claps his hands.)* God, we've made some inroads. Dug in deep. You got a better sense of who you are, and your place in the universe. At ease! Now how do you feel?

LEN: Crazy, but it did clear my head. Maybe the blood supply opens new synapses....

ROY: I said it did. If you'd clean the wax outta your ears...

LEN: Listen...I'm going along with all this because it's the path of least resistance. But don't think I'm doing it for you!

SHEILA: *(Hissing, butting in)* Len, don't be confrontational!

BEV: The husbands never get along.

SHEILA: *(Lowest, to LEN)* This is no time for a show of male dominance! Humor him! We have to get his guard down....

LEN: I can't take much more, Sheila! *(To ROY)* Don't think I'm doing all this for you!

SHEILA: Ssssh!

LEN: You think you can break me! But you can't! You can't break me....

SHEILA: *(Whispering to BEV, ROY)* He's tired and hungry; he doesn't know what he's saying....

LEN: *(Defying* ROY *and* SHEILA*)* You can't break me!
I have my own strength! It comes from being Already
Broken!

ROY: *(Level)* Well spoken. Let's celebrate.... *(He aims the
remote, clicks on Night System.)* Let's make it a Big
Saturday Night!

LEN & SHEILA: What the....

*(The unit is plunged into a midnight system. Constellations,
the sliver of a quarter-moon. Night sounds: Crickets,
bullfrogs. ROY, becoming excited, swings up to his rings.)*

ROY: Look at that sky! You got to see the stars to know
where you are! There's Jupiter! Mighty Jupiter! You'd
never see this in New York. Not so clear and bright!
City light bleaches out heaven! Ain't right!

LEN: *(Whispering to* SHEILA*)* I might be able to grab him
as he goes by, and bring him down....

SHEILA: Not yet... Wait for the signal... He's got to burn
himself out.

ROY: When I die, I fly! Right up to them stars, right
between them dippers! My soul gonna pop right out of
my mouth...I picture it as a bubble...small and round....

BEV: *(Whispering to* LEN, SHEILA*)* You're starting to like
him, aren't you?

SHEILA: It's not a question of liking, it's a question
of what's feasible, and what's not. Sweetie, I know
you better than you know yourself, and I know that,
eventually, you'll snap out of this, and thank me....
So why put off what's inevitable? Come with us.
Leave him. He's some kind of sickie who couldn't
make it in the outside world....

BEV: Maybe the outside world wasn't worthy of him!
When he was in the military, wherever he was
deployed... His own men tried to kill him.

SHEILA: I can't say I'm surprised.

BEV: No one has understood him but me! No one can see but me!

LEN: *(To BEV)* No, no...I see...many of the things he says, I can see...he's not...without feeling....

BEV: Oh, Len, he's capable of such great beauty, I could weep!

(ROY lands, uses his remote.)

ROY: Listen up? Music Appreciation!

(BEV indicates to others— "see". Tape of Tom T Hall plays: "I Love— I love...Little baby ducks...old pickup trucks... slow movin' trains and rain...")

ROY: Hey, this ain't half-terrible, is it? You want to dance? (SHEILA, *fazed, moves automatically toward him, as does* BEV. LEN *keeps trying to get* SHEILA's *attention: Should he attack?)*

ROY: Oh, I can't dance. You two go on! Hell, I've got two left feet.... I'd kill you.... You two girls, go on...!

(BEV, SHEILA begin to dance. ROY switches on another tape—Hernando's Hideaway.)

ROY: Cha-cha. *(To group)* Hey, I'm going to crack us some cold ones.... We'll have a Moonlight party.... Maybe later we can open up your wine....

SHEILA: Oh, please!

ROY: And we'll have ourselves a spread! What're you all in the mood for? Chinese? We'll have the Hunan Supper, that's the Special Supper!

LEN: *(Under his breath to SHEILA as she dances past)* Sheila!

(He signals: "When?" She mimes: "Soon".)

ROY: *(Displaying the Hunan cube as he puts it in the oven)* Whole Striped Bass—Hunan Style! Better put it in

now—this guy takes awhile to bloat up.... Wait'll
you taste him, though—you'll think you're at a great
Chinese joint.... I got some Chinese beer to go with it....

(ROY *goes for a beer, as women dance.*)

ROY: Hey, hey, Mighty Len: How about a cold one?

LEN: Thanks, but no thanks. I'm trying to keep a clear
head. Go ahead, don't mind me. I'll just concentrate.

(ROY *shoots a look: he does mind.* ROY *kicks back, watching
the women dance.*)

ROY: *(Drinking beer)* Hey, this is cozy, huh?

LEN: *(Totally absorbed)* Oh, yeah, it's great.

ROY: *(Firm whisper to* LEN*)* Hey, Len, Mighty Len...
This is a party. You can do that later.

(LEN *ignores him.*)

ROY: *(To women)* Looking good, girls! *(To* LEN*)* Come
on, Len, we're having a good time, here! I am too.

(SHEILA *begins to look overheated, enjoying her dance,
but perspiring.*)

SHEILA: Oh, I'm hot!

(ROY *zeroes in, dancing toward her.*)

ROY: *(Under his breath)* Oh, I know you are. *(Aloud)*
Wooo! It's getting steamy in here! *(Pointed, toward* LEN*)*
Three of us, laughin' an' dancin' an' drinkin'...
Here, have some of the...for-real hard stuff....

(ROY *passes a bottle of tequila,* BEV *eyes* SHEILA:
What's going on?)

ROY: Woo! Listen to that beat. Hey, Mighty Mamba
Mighty Cha! Cha! Oh, man, what a night.... *(He dances
harder over to* LEN, *lowers his voice.*) Len, you don't want
to spoil the party?

LEN: Oh, no. You all go on. I just want to get in a bit more before I call it a night.

ROY: The thesis?

LEN: I don't want to lose it!

(ROY *crowds* LEN, *peering at him.*)

ROY: *(Mild, curious)* How long you been wearing glasses, Len?

LEN: Since fifth grade. I probably needed them sooner but I thought they were unflattering for my face....

ROY: They *are* unflattering, Len. And the glass is giving off a glare that is irritating to my own eyes. When I look at you...I see myself, all twisted up. Maybe you don't need them anymore....

(ROY *takes* LEN's *glasses.*)

LEN: Oh, no! I do!

(ROY *crushes the glasses.*)

ROY: Maybe you just think you do. What would you do if they just accidentally broke? There's a way to make substitute lenses. Think about sight. Think about light. You can figure it out. Why be dependent on glasses all your life?

LEN: *(Wailing, to his wife)* Sheila!

(As SHEILA *crosses to* LEN, ROY *returns to* BEV, *who is reacting to the glasses-smashing: she trembles.*)

LEN: *(Hissing to* SHEILA*)* Look! He's getting wild.

SHEILA: Just a minute! Give me one minute!

LEN: We better do something now, Sheila!

SHEILA: Len, don't argue with me. *(Sweeter)* Come on, hon...

LEN: *(With his last ounce of civilization)* Well, all right.

(SHEILA *mimes: "Wait for this signal"—the hand-chop.*
LEN *nods.*)

ROY: *(Stroking* BEV*)* What're you shiverin' and quiverin'
about?

BEV: I feel cold.

ROY: Well, assume the position for preventing
hypothermia. Survival Drill! Bev! Len! I think
you should do this too.... Lie down on the floor.
Opposing directions...Bev—your feet in Len's armpits.
Len, your feet in Bev's armpits ...*bare* feet!

LEN: I'd rather not....

ROY: *(Rational tone, but drunk)* I'm teaching you these
skills for your own good, Len. This could save your life
one day. It's one of the for-real great ones....

*(*LEN*, *BEV *assume the position.)*

ROY: All right. Imagine, if you will, you're in below-
zero conditions. You're going to freeze to death if you
don't do armpits. In two hours, your toes will be rigid,
black, beyond recall. The only cure is amputation!
(Correcting the pose) Belly to butt!

*(*LEN*, *BEV *assume tighter pose.)*

ROY: Now, ain't that cozy? That's not half-terrible, is it?
Now, lock into that. Don't move a muscle. It is now
nineteen-hundred hours. You are to remain until
twenty-hundred hours. You will know when you hear
this whistle.... *(He leads his whistle up the deep valley of*
SHEILA*'s cleavage, upward to outline her mouth...he inserts*
the whistle between her lips.) This is the whistle. Stay in
position, until you hear this whistle.... *(Smile)* Sheila and
I are going into the other room to have sex.

(Catching their response)

ROY: Well, would you rather I *lied* and said we were just
going to talk?

(He switches on his electronic Sex Program: A fire blazes on the illuminating screen: tongues of flame, leaping upward. Music—Bruce Springsteen, "I'm On Fire" plays. ROY has turned, to head into bedroom. SHEILA pauses to reassure LEN, BEV.)

SHEILA: *(Reassuring whisper)* Don't worry. I can handle him.

(She follows ROY into bedroom. ROY has zipped into shower stall, instantly reappears, posed in the doorway. He tilts his heads a sexual invitation. The backlighting, golden, from the shower, should inspire recollection of his famous "corona." SHEILA, weakened by the sight, and violently aroused, falls backward on the bed. ROY stands before her, and, with a smile, begins to caress her. He rubs his own cheek, with her hand, then strokes her legs. He raises her legs so that she holds them high, fully extended: she appears to hang by her heels, her ankles locked behind his head.)

ROY: *(Erotic whisper)* Mighty Sheila. Mighty Sheila.

(In the other room, LEN and BEV hold their shocked pose for a moment, their heads raised in jealous alarm. Then BEV pops into sit-up position, then so does LEN. Silently, LEN embraces BEV, offering his reassurances There is nothing they can do about their defected mates. In the dim bedroom, SHEILA moans: their dark, entwined bodies turn.... Lights flash on/off. Whistle blows. ROY stands by bed, SHEILA lies on covers, spent.)

ROY: *(Calling to living room)* At ease! *(Soft)* Quiet Time.

SHEILA: *(In a sexual semi-coma)* Uh...baby. Come here.

(ROY doesn't move. His voice is neutral.)

ROY: What?

SHEILA: Would you do something for me?

ROY: What?

SHEILA: *(Whisper)* I can't move. Could you bring my suitcase in here? The big brown one? And the little plastic makeup case?

ROY: They're all right where they are. I'm going to wash up. Catch you later.

SHEILA: But it was incredible!

ROY: *(As he heads into john)* Always is, darlin'.

(ROY vanishes into shower stall: door snaps shut. SHEILA braces herself. She rises, shaken, then sees that ROY has left his remote hand control on the bed. She seizes the remote control, tucks it into her brassiere, hides it, and bracing herself, reenters the living room. LEN rises to confront her. BEV sits, stunned, on the sofa.)

LEN: *(With controlled fury)* Was that the plan? I told you—no new nausea, Sheila!?????

SHEILA: He was stronger than I thought. Someone had to mollify him. *(Beat)* I'm sorry.

LEN: Damn right, you're sorry. You are sorry! You owe Bev an apology! You are a guest in this house!

SHEILA: *(To BEV)* I'm sorry. He held my hands down.

BEV: And you told me he was out of the question!

SHEILA: *(Dazed)* I saw the corona. That was...amazing.

LEN: *(Pacing the room, is caught short by this remark)* I knew we were having problems, but an infidelity....

SHEILA: *(Offhand)* We were separated....

LEN: In the next room! This is...a new low! This is bottom?

SHEILA: *(A bit humbled)* There really is a corona.

BEV: I kept telling you.

LEN: Does this mean...you want to keep seeing him?

SHEILA: Keep seeing him!? No, it's...over. Forget about it, Len. I have.

LEN: You don't forget something like this...an *affair*.

SHEILA: You're overreacting: It was no big deal. I just hated him so much—I had to work it off!

BEV: *(She bristles.)* When I think: I *cleaned* before you got here.

SHEILA: *(Consoling, to* LEN, *who turns away from her)* Look. I was with him...for what...nine minutes? What was it? Some slick passage through my body?

*(*LEN *is contorting.)*

SHEILA: I've been with you for nine *years*. That's what counts. I love you. Look! *(She whips out the remote control, aims it at the Vista Wall, and immediately produces a downward roll, as if she has broken Horizontal Hold.)*

*(*ROY, *whistling, re-enters.)*

BEV: *(To* SHEILA*)* You...I heard you moan!

ROY: *(Casually)* Yeah, when she went over... God, these females, can't get them started without a lot of fine tuning, then can't get them to stop. She was giving off the scent. That's how come her voice has been going high...yeah, she was buckin' like a bronco.... *(He sees the rolling Vista.)* What the hell's been going on in here?

BEV: *(Turning on him)* You let her see the corona! That was for us! Between us!

ROY: I only liked her 'cause she was your friend. She kind of reminded me of you. Only you're better than her. You fit me better than her. When I got to know her, I hated her so much I had to work it off....

BEV: I have my limits!

ROY: You want a divorce!

BEV: Yeah! *(He gets the divorce papers, stamp.)*

ROY: Well, you throw in the towel kind of quick, don't you? You never cared about me at all, did you? You just wanted to get married again.

BEV: That's absurd. I loved you.

ROY: Loved, huh? Past tense? *(Heartbroken, soft, childish tone)* You never cared, you never fuckin cared.... Nobody ever cared about me...this is no different. I thought I'd try, one time, I was fuckin' at ease here, for the first fuckin' time in my life...I open my heart, I open my house, try to save everybody, show them the way, and nobody gives a shit for me....

(He approaches the stunned CALENDARS, *who have become pinned to the couch.)*

ROY: What do I need you here for? I'm sick of your face...I'm sick of your wife, feeding her face. She's had a man's year's worth of ice cream in one night...and are you even chippin' in? Are you even chippin' in?

SHEILA: *(Hissing)* Tell him, Len, tell him what we spent for gas....

LEN: That's not relevant....

BEV: *(Low)* He's in a mood: I've never seen this side before....

ROY: It's not the money, it's the thought. Did you ever fuckin' think, did you ever fuckin' think, maybe I could use a little cooperation?

LEN: Huh?

ROY: You got that sigh, it's going off in my head like a bomb. *(Sigh)* Huh. I can't walk cross my own living room without tripping over all a your shit. Did you ever offer to help me? Sure, when I asked. But did it ever come from you? Did you ever stop and fuckin' think, maybe I'd have liked an occasional "Thank you" ?

LEN: Thank you!

ROY: There's one thing I won't tolerate in my home, and that's sarcasm. "This kills it for me."

BEV: Roy, don't do this to yourself! You can afford to be more generous!

ROY: I want some shit from you, I'll squeeze your head. *(Beat)* And don't go talking about me behind my back! I'm not letting your fucked-up friends stay here again! I've had it with them! They can come and socialize for an hour or two, then: Out! Next time, they can make their own accommodations. Let them pay for a motel! I'm not running a Hilton here!

LEN: A what?

ROY: I don't like the sound of your breathing. It tears at my ears. *(He moves in closer to* SHEILA.*)* And your wife has done something terrible to my tool:

(SHEILA *starts.)*

ROY: She probably gave me some kind of New York clap, and I went into the dirtiest whores in Hong Kong.... *(His tone is increasingly tender, chivalrous.)* bareback...and I never got sick, always passed the blood test...clean as a whistle...I broke through crusts to get into them, and they never took my money, either. They were wonderful women; I wish I had them now....

(SHEILA, *furious, signals* LEN: *the hand-chop.)*

SHEILA: Kill him!

LEN: Just-lemme-alone-in-peace-and-quiet...
Just-lemme-alone-in-peace-and-quiet...

(SHEILA *yowls: wide-mouth, joining* BEV, *in full babyish bawl.)*

ROY: Quit yer bawling, you'll give me a headache.... *(He goes to* SHEILA.*)* This is you. *(He goes, jeering, to* BEV.*)*

And you, you're going to seed on me. Turning into a lardo. You used to lcok sexy. You could put on something that would disguise yourself a bit...have a heart! *(He looks at them all.)* Well, that's it. Fuck it. Forget the party! You—assholes—are going! Start packing!

(SHEILA starts packing; LEN runs for his toiletries.)

SHEILA: Believe me, I can't wait....

ROY: Yeah, toots... Your vacation is over.... Your two weeks is going to go by before you know it, and you're getting only one event—out of here! I'm speeding up the timer, and you're going out on your butt....

(Rooster crows. Picture straightens, but shows The Great Salt Lake.)

ROY: What's all this? Everything's been fucked with.... Where's my crickets.... And my little bullfrog?

SHEILA: *(Working the remote)* Make it go by... Make it go...

(ROY sees red when he sees her with the remote.)

SHEILA: Just open the goddamned door for me....

ROY: I'd love to.... But now you've messed up my equipment! You hadn't done enough damage! You come here, uninvited and louse up everything....

LEN: *(Patting BEV)* It's all right. I appreciate your saying that to me. We had some...nice moments...the dinner....

(ROY, meanwhile, is struggling.)

ROY: It's jammed.

SHEILA: *(Snapping her suitcases shut)* Open the door for me.

ROY: I'm trying to....

(He forces the lever: It breaks off in his hand. They all stare: trying to grasp the significance.)

ROY: Holy shit.

LEN: But, but...it can't open without that....
Is that the problem?

ROY: The problem is: we're fucked...we are really
fucked....

SHEILA: You putz! Well, that's just great. So now what?

(ROY *collapses on his sofa.*)

ROY: *(A bit bitter)* Make yourselves at home. *Mea casa is
sua casa....*

LEN: Forever?

ROY: *(Computing)* For two man years for the four of us...

(BEV *begins to act out, spinning violently, throwing off her
clothes.*)

BEV: I'm not staying. *(She runs, stripping off clothes,
to the kitchen, and opens the air-duct grate. She then turns,
grabs a can of Crisco and begins to smear her bikini-clad body
with the thick white fat)*

SHEILA: *(Ranting to herself)* Two man years....

ROY: *(Ranting to himself)* I'm sorry I ever saw you....
(BEV) ...I'm sorry I ever put it in you...I should have
known a city woman would give me a hard time....

SHEILA: He's a sickle, a mean little sickle...who couldn't
make it in the outside world. Oh, he can be a king down
here.

LEN: *(Soft)* I think he's very...troubled.

(BEV *grabs the divorce stamp, attacks* ROY; *stamping
"DIVORCED" on his forehead.*)

BEV: Just get one thing straight: This is my divorce!
So long, soldier!

(*She spins, wriggles up the air duct.* ROY *tracks her.*)

ROY: Babe? Babe! You don't want to go. You don't want to really fuckin' go.... *(Soft)* All couples have fights.... *(Sweet, heartfelt)* Love don't die so fast, no matter what we say—hey...I'll be what you want me to be! I'll do what you want me to do! I'll be nice to your friends...I'm a nice guy!

SHEILA: Shut up. Where does this vent come out?

ROY: God knows. Somewhere in the middle of the fuckin' desert...It could go halfway to Vegas....

LEN: *(To ROY)* You know how it is, if you just share a bed, you give in to the body heat, and the next thing you know: You're clinging to someone who.... *(He checks with SHEILA)* has different politics.

(ROY marches to doorway where SHEILA is poised to enter)

ROY: *(To LEN)* I'll stay in there with her, man; it seems like the only *(He searches for word.)* solution. *(Looks at SHEILA)* It's a tough row to hoe, but I don't see no alternative. *(Lower, to SHEILA)* Don't get it in your head I'll marry you, I won't. A) I just got divorced. B) You marry someone, you just get burned.

SHEILA: Marry! Marry you? Don't make me laugh. If your brain was as big as your dick, I wouldn't marry you.

LEN: *(Head bobbing, as he tries to track this conversation)* " As big as his..."... *(New tone)* Oh, Sheila! Sheila! Don't say everything that comes into your head. He isn't me. You better modify it a bit.

ROY: I don't like lip.

SHEILA: And I don't kowtow....

ROY: *(To LEN)* Woooo! I don't even like this one much. *(Thinking aloud)* But I'm going to need a tension reliever.

SHEILA: So you don't get headaches?

ROY: As I recall, we were a pretty good fit.

SHEILA: "Fit" ? You don't say "fit"...*Shoes* fit. *Clothes* fit.
You don't go into a woman and talk about fit...
People don't fit!

ROY: They sure don't.... *(He blocks her move to the
bedroom.)* And that's my room in there.

SHEILA: Well, rot in it! I'm getting out! If I have to claw
my way out.... *(She raids cutlery drawers.)* There must be
a screwdriver, some sharp knives....

ROY: You touch them wires, there'll be hell to pay.

LEN: Sheila, you know nothing about electronics.

SHEILA: I know I have to go! I have to get out of here
before I lose my mind...Stay ire here with you...Hah!
Live under *your* rule...just because you think you're
God's gift to women and have some magical thing
between your legs and...you have no friends!

*(As she rants, SHEILA strikes live wires: Loud sizzle. Sparks.
she is electrocuted. There is a blackout. A short time later.
Lights rise to only one-third strength, and fluctuate, as if
during a brownout. This power surge and ebb condition has
been in effect since the demise of SHEILA. The screen shows
the Hawaiian Sunset, and the broken stereo plays,* Love to
Love You, Baby. *LEN and ROY are conducting a funeral
service. Both men look wasted: ROY in even deeper shock
than LEN. ROY writes "SHEILA" namecard on morgue
drawer)*

ROY: God. I know. It is an awful thing. Busted the Beta
Max when she went...Took it with her. They're charcoal
now....

(Seeing LEN sniffle)

ROY: I know, oh, God, I know...I know you were split,
but that don't change your feelings as much as you
thought it would, does it?

(LEN *bobs his head in agreement.*)

ROY: I felt like you do now when Bev left me....
'Cause divorce is different but...loss is loss. We didn't
get along either toward the end, but that didn't mean
we didn't fuckin' care....

LEN: Could we have more appropriate music?
(*He looks up: he wears homemade lenses—eyeglasses
made from punctured tinfoil, with pinpoint pupils.*)

ROY: I had a whole funeral system. Amazing Grace.
Rain. Now it's shot; it's all shot, gone...

(*Screen flashes Antarctic vista*)

LEN: (*Moved*) Oh, God, why weren't you like this when
I first got here?

ROY: I ain't the one who's been changin'.... (*He holds his
head.*)

LEN: Hey, we could really kick some ideas around....
We-can start a whole new schedule....

ROY: What the fuck for? (*To himself*) My head's crackin'
opens It's The Big One....

(*The lights flicker ominously.*)

ROY: And we're losin' the power....

LEN: Ummm...we do seem to be...but you can run this
place with your feet!

ROY: (*Very bitter*) Wasn't that "neat"?

LEN: Hey, look, you were the guy who said:
"Don't give up now, give up later..."

ROY: That was earlier in the evening.

LEN: Well, the end is not quite in sight.... If you run,
the Ped-O-Power can keep us going for....

ROY: "Four man years for the two of us..." We're going to die down here, we're going to fuckin' die down here...it's just going to take awhile....

LEN: Somebody might think of coming to look for us.

ROY: *(Eyes rolling heavenward)* Yeah, it says "Sewer."

LEN: You know who I bet could find us?

ROY: Nobody...

LEN: MasterCard. Visa. I was way overdue. I haven't met my minimum in so long, if my thesis is correct, they'll come after me....

ROY: You got that much faith in the system?

LEN: *That* part of it. You can always trust your creditors: They won't forget you. And one thing I've learned since coming down here: I can have complete faith in what I fear!

(Lights flicker more ominously)

ROY: I don't even know how long you been here.

LEN: Well, I arrived on Friday night...and I know we were well into Saturday when...well, things broke down....

ROY: So my whole future is going to be Sunday.... Like an endless—Sunday. Sunday, around three, with nothing good on T V, *(He studies the screen.)* I had a really sharp picture. *(He guzzles the beer, burps.)* An' you hate me.

LEN: I never said that.

ROY: *(Very babyish)* You hate me.

LEN: I don't think in terms of "hate".

ROY: But it's got to be in yer gut every time you look at me.... You come here...and stay against your will... I make it with your wife....

LEN: My ex-wife.

ROY: Be that as it may, I got a little rough....

LEN: I resented you, I admit that....

ROY: And then I cause her to...expire....

LEN: That was an accident.

ROY: Yeah, well, my whole life's an accident now....

LEN: Awww... There's an inner agony, isn't there?
I should have spotted that the second I saw you...
overcompensating. So much fortification...
only someone so scared would....

ROY: (Starting to cry) I was orderin' you around, too...
I wasn't as hospitable as I might a been....

LEN: Listen, it's true you were overbearing, you had
an affair with my wife, my ex-wife, and accidentally
caused her to expire, but I never said I didn't enjoy
your company...You ran a tight ship. You had a
sophisticated system...I never liked to depend on the
technology; I admit, I slipped into it.... You even had a
kind of vision.... Something for. the Body. Something
for the Brain..."

ROY: "Something for the Soul," don't remind me....
(Whisper) Len, I don't like it here. It's...small.

LEN: Hey, hey, hey, it's not that bad...Well, all right...
it is. But this is so bad...it's bracing! My mind keeps
racing! There are...no distractions. Don't you see?
Knowing how bleak it is, can be...a kind of exhilaration!
I'm discovering new levels to the bottom! God, you just
can go down, down, down.... There's a kind of rapture
to it, a rapture of depression...God, this is even better
than the torpor I knew back home, in 4-R. I lived in a
depression then, but it couldn't compare to this one.
It was one that I carved out for myself, specifically in
my bed, amidst the bedding that conformed to my own

body: I stayed cocooned in comforters for days, warmed by my own heat, nesting, hibernating in a den of down.... It can get pretty sensuous, erotic even....

ROY: *(Wan)* Sounds like it can lead to an endless wacking off...we called it "choking the chicken" .

LEN: Yes! That can be a part of it! Desire can detonate, quietly, under cover.... And then the mind can soar free—into this...solitary ecstasy! But this...this can be even better than 4-R! The bleakness of this can give you a true rush! A blood song to the brain! Why I can recall whole chunks of Heidegger, and Kierkegaard, too!

ROY: *(Mumbling)* I haven't had sex for over an hour.

LEN: The energy will go somewhere else! Come on, don't you see? What more can we ask for? Than that our fate be...well, singular? We're the only ones doing this! It can be *new*! Between me and you!

(Lights rise to half-strength. LEN is alone. Screen shows a moon rise. Lighting is lunar,

LEN: Roy? Huh? This is no time to play games... Yoo-hoo...I see you.... *(He searches.)* Where the h?

(LEN executes a quick search, then, on impulse, approaches the morgue drawers. he yanks open the drawer: ROY pops up, in sit-up position)

LEN: *(Scream, gasp)* Awwwwgggggh!

ROY: *(Rapid-fire)* I'm checking out. Ate the suicide pie. It wasn't halfterrible. There's no cramping, Len. I can't stay. Life's too short, that's for sure, but Sunday afternoon's *tooooo* long. I'll be happier dead. Goddamn, I know I will. There's got to be a world, after this one, not for everyone, but for some...and I'm one. Don't you go off the deep end. Think of eight man years for you, instead of four for the two of us. Make yourself at home. *(He keels backward, dead in the drawer)*

LEN: *(Studying the body, as he would regard a dead pet: babyish regret)* Awwwwh. *(He shuts drawer— expedient.)* Boy oh boy. *(He fills in name-card.)* " Mighty Roy."

LEN: *(With stunned, excited pauses)* Boy oh boy. Woo...

(The microwave open timer tings. Reflexively, LEN withdraws the cooked Hunan fish dinner. he carries it to the table, does not sit down, but begins to circle, in ever-increasing momentum.)

LEN: Un-unh. I'm not going. Not like this. Not down here. I have a feel for how I'll go. The way everyone in my family went...We linger. Extensive hospital stays. So as not to deprive distant cousins of something to do on the weekends. Oh, yeah. That's how it'll be. This has nothing to do with me. This was his idea. I was just visiting.

(The music has started. LEN hums as he circles. The defective sound system emits day and night noises. Birds chirp and crickets cheep. LEN runs onto the treadmill, trots in place. His eyes light with a fevered surprise: Behind him, on the screen, we see a hot, synthetic sunrise. LEN's pace quickens, as the room brightens...he runs faster, faster, fueled by an ecstatic delusion. he smiles, as if to someone else. The final spotlight illuminates him: a lone man running in a world out-of-whack, both the moon and the sun at his back.)

LEN: *(Sings; manic, upbeat rendition)* Why don't you love me like you used to do? Why did you toss me out like a worn-out shoe? My hair's still curly, and my eyes are still blue.... Oh, why don't you love me, like you used to do?

(Blackout)

END OF PLAY

www.ingramcontent.com/pod-product-compliance
Lightning Source LLC
Chambersburg PA
CBHW052203090426
42741CB00010B/2391